Maps

Maps

Five Leaves Publications
www.fiveleaves.co.uk

Maps

Edited by Ross Bradshaw

Published and reprinted in 2011
by Five Leaves Publications
PO Box 8786, Nottingham NG1 9AW
www.fiveleaves.co.uk

ISBN: 9781907869242

Five Leaves acknowledges
financial support from
Arts Council England

Five Leaves is represented
to the trade by Turnaround
and distributed by Central Books

Cover design: Richard Hollis

Typeset and designed by
Four Sheets Design and Print

Printed in Great Britain

Contents

Introduction

Maps is the first in a series of annual journals, drawing together essays from some of those who write regularly or irregularly for Five Leaves, together with other authors in our periphery. Some of the essays are "from the vaults", some from work in progress while others were commissioned for this collection.

Since Five Leaves began, in 1996, there have been suggestions that the press should focus on one or two niches. That might make sense in marketing terms but publishing across a range of subjects is more interesting and brings in many writers we would not otherwise have worked with, or got to know. For some time now we have had a journal in mind that brings together authors, from widely different traditions, writing on one theme. We requested or commissioned material on the broad subject of "maps", but which also relate to Five Leaves' areas of interest. In this issue there are essays on social history, Roman Britain, London fiction, poetry, Catalonia, travel writing, and Five Leaves' hometown of Nottingham, all areas which rub along happily on our overall list.

We are grateful to those who contributed.

This collection is dedicated to the late Colin Ward, whose work was a major influence on Five Leaves. Colin was an anarchist, a writer and friend. We published several books written or jointly written by him: on allotments, on the history of squatting, on British holiday camps and on the plotlands of south-east England. We hope that Colin would have seen this journal as following in the tradition of his own life and work.

The next two journals will be on "crime" and "utopia".

Ross Bradshaw
Five Leaves
August 2011

7

Mr Tapscott
Iain Sinclair

Discovering that most of the kitchen staff, waiters and chambermaids, in the high days of the Midland Hotel at Morecambe, the era epitomised by a photograph of Lord and Lady Docker descending the staircase in the supreme complacency of their evening wear, came from Liverpool, I knew that a return to the City of Culture was inevitable. I had an arrangement to walk through Toxteth with John Davies, the long-distance vicar, the man who had tramped the M62 from Hull to Liverpool, posting blogs from alien territory, testing himself in his distance from home.

We had met, once before, in Cheltenham. John invited me to take part in the Greenbelt Festival, which happened over an August weekend on the racecourse, and which involved a cast of many thousands camping in tents, feeding from numerous stalls, and primed to enjoy themselves whatever the weather. Having been too long in this town, at boarding school, I tended to keep well away, as from a relatively open prison, experienced, endured, even enjoyed, but done with, finished: another self, not eliminated, but buried without regret in an unmarked grave. I'd never been part of a large-scale festival, so I took up the offer of a room in a Thistle hotel near a major roundabout, alongside the GCHQ listening station, a secure and sinister new town of huts, bunkers, masts, and apartments for career spooks. Banal off-road architecture surrounds the doughnut of the inner circle, the hooped structure where global intelligence is gathered. The unmediated babble of the world is processed in a space where you might expect to find a retail park. GCHQ is Gloucestershire's biggest employer. National belt-tightening doesn't begin to lick the sugar from this doughnut. It is awarded, each year, the bulk of the £2.4 billion set aside for Britain's intelligence agencies. On the day when we celebrated the news that we had won the 2012 Olympics, Cheltenham received, by way of an NSA interception, a message from Afghanistan: 'Tomorrow is zero hour'. The next morning, as commuters struggled to work in London, the bombs went off in the Underground. On the day after that, GCHQ completed the translation.

The underlying theme of the festival was Christian. My problem, when confronted by an expectant audience, sitting on the grass, was being carried away by the tent-show revivalist aspect. My pitch was too spiritual. I kept banging on about the pilgrimage aspect, the quest, the journey of the soul. The believers were much more down to earth, socially concerned, having a good time as part of the crowd, processing between stand-up comedians, bands, films, workshops, lectures. The one venue peddling beer was blasphemously signboarded as: The Jesus Arms. I went on after a talk entitled 'Bill Gates, Bono and You'.

John Davies, who appeared with me, spoke of the sense of awe he experienced, standing on a hillside above the M62, 'watching the traffic steadily flowing across the high Pennines like a metallic ribbon glittering in the sunshine'. There was, he acknowledged, a dimension of wonder in the ritualistic process of motorway driving, post-Ballardian sensory enhancement, deep reverie. He spoke of the gospels as a kind of divinely inspired Highway Code. He found my attitude towards this liminal territory, as expressed in *London Orbital*, more critical than his own: he was undergoing, in his foot-foundered exhaustion, an epiphany. The road was a metaphor, the prompt for an unwritten sermon. 'Above Asda, only sky.'

The hiking urban vicar, a compact man, close-cropped, thin-spectacled, smiling, met me on the steps of the Anglican Cathedral. He wore a worker priest's uniform of black shirt and dark anorak, but he had writer's hands.

In his rucksack he carried a copy of *Mr Tapscott*, a self-published poem by the late Bill Griffiths. An inspiration to both of us. Griffiths, with his gift for synthesis, righteous indignation, textual archaeology, was the perfect guide to the condemned terraces of Toxteth, those wide Welsh streets and decommissioned Presbyterian chapels. Bill shaped his poem around the dubious conviction of two men, Ray Gilbert and John Kamara, for the killing of a betting shop manager in March 1981. The spark for the Toxteth riots. 'The bulging world-of-state is a crisis.' The spaces in my dialogue with John Davies, on our tour through layers of Liverpool history, parks, houses and handsome flats once owned by Adrian Henri or Roger McGough, are filled with the growling resonance of Bill's unheard voice. Patterns of language, so generously set before those who need them, are an absolute: they cohere, they are not extinguished. To fix or interpret sections of the ring-bound poem moved us along, from named address to park, to café. 'One hemisphere of the marvellous,' Bill wrote of the streets through which we were trudging. My own copy of the poem, I notice on returning home, has a Griffiths drawing of the Liver Bird, hand-coloured, with splashes of green waves.

Walking alongside John Davies is a journey through absence, neighbourhood enterprises on Rialto Corner laid over the burnt-out traces of the original riots. 'A vast area of working-class terraces reduced from a living, active community to a tinned-up wilderness by one signature sweep of John Prescott's hand,' Davies said. In Princes Road the red-brick chapel has been made into a secure island by a fence that carries the testimonials of the expelled parishioners. I was interested to note that the ubiquitous painted crocodile of Hackney Wick's Olympic Park, that symbol of devouring economic imperatives, has waddled into Liverpool 8. NO MORE DEMOLITION, NO MORE BULL. DREAM ON FOR REGENERATION. Cartoon-graffiti terraces have smiling faces in the windows, where the surviving streets have chipboard. No blue plaque on the house where Ringo Starr grew up. When a Beatles tour bus pauses at the end of the road, nobody gets out. In Bethnal Green, similar properties, on tighter streets, now sell for half-a-million pounds.

On Lodge Lane we stop for sandwiches in a bright new café called MT BELLY's. The mugs of tea comes free. I'm intrigued by what Bill Griffiths has to say about 'the attempt to raise a new set of myths, things that were neutral but archetypal'. If we fail to follow the poet's example, and to hammer out a mythology of our own, we are lost. In Toxteth, we encountered nothing but friendliness, an active interest in our presence, as we wandered the quiet streets and deserted parks. The man in the café, launching a business, fresh paint, overloaded sandwiches, topped-up mugs, hovered over our discussion. I placed my recorder on the table to capture the story of John's hike from Hull to Liverpool. 'Bill Griffiths,' he said, 'talked about how history and literature have been colonised by certain big names. He works to reclaim it. It's good to be sitting in Lodge Lane and wondering if Bill perched here himself.'

I've always had a feeling about the M62. It's been a motorway I have travelled a lot, through visiting family and friends in different parts of the north. I've enjoyed the journey, by car. I could wonder about things I could see, landmarks, just outside the boundaries of the motorway: churches, civic-looking buildings, heavy industry. These things started to raise questions in my mind. I wanted to walk to get closer to those sites. I'd done a lot of urban walks, it was the urban thing I was interested in.

I didn't see the Will Alsop thing of the SuperCity as being workable. I was so concerned to look at specific details of each place. I was finding the differences between places, more than the similarities. The Alsop idea doesn't reflect the cultural reality. The interesting thing is to walk through the new developments and to see how individuals or small groups, small collectives, have started to make their own archives of the places where they live — with little bits of graffiti, or structural adjustments to signage.

I'd never been to Hull before. I enjoyed Hull. It seemed to be that bit apart from all the other cities on the M62 journey. It has worked at its identity. I was interested to note that the docklands development, the waterside, was built a long time ago. The original development was carried out in the early '80s. They started in Liverpool in the late '80s. They thought it out for themselves in Hull, rather than latching on to someone else's development.

Sometimes it's good to get lost, but sometimes it isn't. I got lost in Leeds, a very dark seedy corner of Leeds, and couldn't find my way out. I had maps with me and couldn't read them because there was no light anywhere. It was a red light area. The only people I could find were high on drugs. It got a bit scary.

I don't know anything about flora and fauna, I'm a city person. I did enjoy walking the Pennines. I spent a day with a farmer. He farmed around the area where the motorway splits in two. I anticipated, wrongly, that he would not have liked it because it was a busy motorway ripping through his land, but in fact all the farmers welcomed the road because it made them accessible.

I didn't know Manchester at all. Another element of my walk was seeing ghosts: certainly in Ancoats, where I was with a friend who had lived there for a long time. He didn't use the word ghost, he was talking about lives that had been lived in that community. He could still see those people and those places. When he looked at the closed-down pubs, he could picture the people who were once sitting in them.

I met people on the road. One guy was walking it because he wanted to connect all the Rugby League grounds, which are mainly along the M62. I did get tired. By the time I reached the outskirts of Liverpool, I just wanted to get home. My legs were gone.

I finished by walking through the arena of my childhood, Crosby Beach. I knocked at my parents' door and we went together to the beach. It was a real sense of homecoming. I hadn't planned it that way. It was quite emotional to realise how much home meant to me. I used to play on Crosby Beach as a kid. And I remember seeing the changes down there, the sandhills going up.

I like the Gormley figures. I think they're doing what I've done often in the past, which is to stand looking at the view: a wide-open sea. They have a nice gentle presence, really. There was a lot of resistance at first, with a lot of

13

people lobbying, particularly those who used the water, like powerboat users. The placement of the figures meant they couldn't use that stretch of water anymore. But the figures have grown on people. They have attracted people to the area.

I finished my three months with a month putting all the words together. I realised that what was important to me, reflecting back, was the writing. The writing was as important as the walk. You construct the world as you go.

I returned to Morecambe to make the walk across the bay, in quest of other ghosts, the drowned cockle pickers. There were prohibitions everywhere: MORECAMBE BAY COCKLE BED CLOSURES. Notices dated from April 2006. Cockling had been suspended until further notice. You don't wait for the tide to retreat and then set off, unaccompanied, across those treacherous sands; you sign on with an official guide. I had expected half a dozen fellow pilgrims, not a Cecil B. DeMille mob, packing the Arnside shoreline, waiting expectantly for their Moses to part the Red Sea. It was an awesome spectacle, that afternoon, hundreds of us, setting off under low cloud, hammered by sudden, special-effects showers. A gnarled prophet called Cedric, cleft stick in hand, trousers rolled, led us on the four-hour hike to Kents Bank. He marshalled his strung-out flock with a whistle. Sandals slung around neck, jeans sodden, I stuck close to our leader as he surged forward at a good clip. The multitude spread out, small children dragged and dawdled, before being hoisted on to the shoulders of their parents. Shaggy dogs wallowed in salt-sticky puddles. We left the land a long way behind. Caterpillar treads of orange Bay Search tractors emerged from a broad rivulet and diminished in the direction of a remote horizon. Amphibious vehicles marked RESCUE alerted us to the unpredictable nature of a place where walkers could very quickly become swimmers.

Cedric sounded a shrill blast, to line us up, on the edge of a channel where the sea had rushed in. As we waded through, we felt not only the strength of the current but the unpleasant sensation of sand eels banging against our naked legs. I took the chance to have a quick word with this man who walked alone, retracing his own footprints, never looking back to confirm that the tribe was still at his heels.

'It was three miles over there.' He pointed with his stick. 'The cockle pickers were on a high sandbank with a fast-flowing river on either side. They had no chance.'

The money earned, £15 for three sacks of cockles, was less than the potential wages to be made sweating in the kitchens of a Manchester restaurant. Or peddling pirated DVDs around mean streets. The gang bosses took their cut and charged for accommodation and food.

Rain slashing down, we slithered through a channel of blue-grey mud, before crossing dunes held together with coarse grass, and achieving firm ground. Our fellow pilgrims, seeking release, rushed into private woodland to piss against innocent trees.

Britain's Lost Cricket Grounds
Chris Arnot

Introduction

Imagine what it would have been like to have been at the Central Ground on the idyllically named Priory Meadow in Hastings on a fine afternoon when Sussex were at home. Hear the cry of gulls hovering overhead or swooping on to the outfield before fleeing in a flap from a square cut cracked by Ted Dexter at his most imperious. Smell the whiff of briny on the breeze as Imran Khan hurtled in from the Sea End. See the sun's rays glinting on the windows of elegant boarding houses; their owners peering out anxiously as Tony Greig hit four consecutive sixes, including one that cleared the stand at square leg.

Sussex were playing Warwickshire at the time and, as one who spent his formative years at Edgbaston, I might have enjoyed the fifth ball even more. Greig was caught on the long-on boundary by Dennis Amis for 226. Note the 'might have'. I wasn't there at the time, the mid-'70s. Nor did I see Dexter at Hastings in the '60s or Imran in the '80s. The first time I clapped eyes on the Central Ground was in the early '90s when it was already earmarked to be built upon by a large shopping centre (named Priory Meadow, needless to say).

Now you don't have to be a cricket fan to understand that this was a prime example of replacing the distinctive with the bog-standard. Nor do you have to be a member of your local civic society to realise that this turn of events is hardly confined to Hastings. Developers and executives sitting in distant board rooms have found it all too easy to push through plans for soulless malls and precincts, cavernous hypermarkets and edge-of-town retail parks harbouring the same chain stores as everywhere else. While nodding through their applications, toothless local authorities have devised traffic systems of byzantine complexity woven around traffic-free high streets with identikit block paving and street furniture.

Cricket clubs have not been the only victims. Too many family-owned shops, characterful pubs and historic coaching inns have gone the same way. And sometimes cricket clubs have not been victims at all. The dedicated officials who run them have been willing to accept the developer's shilling as a way out of crippling debt. To make way for Tesco or Asda, Barratt or Bovis Homes, they upped stumps and moved. Often they acquired better facilities as a result, albeit in featureless settings, more often than not on corporately owned sports complexes. Some clubs went bust before developers, or anybody else, could make them an offer. Others lost manpower as well as money as players drifted away, seduced by the growing number of alternatives to spending weekend afternoons in the field or in the pavilion, and evenings in the club bar or the nearest pub.

The disappearance of distinctive cricket grounds didn't start in the 1980s; far from it. But the eighties speeded up the process. It was the decade when Britain changed, changed utterly. A terrible duty was born to re-balance the economy. Apparently there was no alternative but to allow mass manufacturing to wither while the commercial, retail and, above all, financial sectors were encouraged to bloom. The patronage that had given birth to country house cricket had largely died away decades before. Now the similarly enlightened self-interest that had bankrolled many a works cricket team began to disappear in turn.

Those paternalistic factory and brewery owners have long gone, as indeed have the dedicated groundsmen they employed. Colliery grounds began to disappear when the pits closed and a way of life was lost forever. As the eighties progressed, state school grounds were built on or given over to less time-consuming sports. And, as the eighties gave way to the nineties and the nineties to the noughties, sky-high house prices forced youngsters to leave the villages they grew up in, depriving the cricket team of fresh talent in the process.

Each lost ground has a story; stirring memories that have been kept alive long after the wicket disappeared under tarmac or bricks and mortar or the year-round pounding of football boots. Each lost ground takes with it a little bit of England; or Wales, or Scotland for that matter. Follow my meandering progress and we'll travel from Dover to Kirkcaldy, Norwich to Newport, calling at overgrown fields, abandoned waste grounds, housing estates, supermarkets and car parks in between.

Don't worry. We won't be dwelling too long in the present. We'll be travelling back to times when these were the sites of cricketing deeds to stir the blood. Of demon bowlers and dashing batsmen, of bruising encounters, harsh words and choice banter. Researching has been a 'labour of love', as my publisher promised it would be. I've met no end of genuine cricket devotees who have gone out of their way to help. Apologies to anyone that I've omitted from the lengthy list of acknowledgements [in the final book] — a list that includes dedicated statisticians, stalwarts of club and village cricket, and a number of old pro's, some of whom were among the sporting heroes of my youth and childhood.

Since their day, the professional game has changed beyond measure in a desperate attempt to appeal to a wider audience. But for some of us there is still a simple pleasure to be had in coming round a bend in a country lane on a Saturday afternoon and pulling over to watch for a while as 13 men in white and two umpires follow the progress of a red ball around a green field on the edge of nowhere in particular. Yes, we have lost many a ground over the past half-century or so. Mercifully, however, there are still more than a few left to remind us that cricket is still threaded through the fabric and the folk memory of the country where this complex yet enthralling game has its roots. And hopefully we can assume that no shopping centres will be built on Broadhalfpenny Down in Hambledon.

Newstead

At one time you only had to whistle down a pit shaft, as the old cliché had it, to bring up a fast bowler. Aptly enough for those in the business of hewing coal, they tended to be fiery characters. Nonetheless, an opposition batsman at Newstead Colliery must have been somewhat taken aback to see the one of the home team's speed merchants hurtling in from what was known as the 'top end' with smoke billowing from his backside.

Dave Atkins was his name and, like quite a few of his team-mates back in the 1960s, he would have done a Saturday-morning shift down the pit before embarking on five hours of cricket. "He liked a couple of pints before the match to lay the dust," recalls long-term wicket keeper Mike Murphy, still stumping at 67, and chairman of what is now Newstead Abbey and Village Cricket Club in the South Notts League. He goes on: "Dave also liked a cigarette and he had a habit of lighting up when he was fielding on the boundary, well away from our captain Billy (Goat Gruff) Radford. Somehow he didn't notice that the tip of his fag had come in contact with the rag that he kept in his back pocket to polish the ball. It was smouldering nicely by the time he came into bowl. Luckily, we managed to put it out before too much damage was caused."

The damage done to mining communities by wholesale pit closures in the 1980s has never been rectified. Here in the heart of what was once Sherwood Forest, little landscaped patches of colliery waste are crested by mock winding wheels marking the spot below which men worked in dirty, difficult and sometimes dangerous conditions. There's one just up the road at Annesley, where Joe Hardstaff junior started work as a pit pony minder when he was fourteen. Twelve years previously, his father, namesake and cricketing mentor 'Old' Joe had moved the family to 25, Fishers Street, Nuncargate, next door but two to the Larwoods.

"Harold and Joe would have played here at one time or another. Bill Voce too," Mike reflects as we park next door to a bowling green, the last remnant of a once-thriving miners' welfare at Newstead. The colliery was closed down in 1987 and cricket ceased soon after. From the front of Mike's four by four, we can see the backs of the new houses that were built on the old ground. "That's where the pavilion was," he says, pointing to a rather soulless semi-detached. "Lovely half-timbered 1930s building it was."

Hot showers were, apparently, provided by coal-fired electricity. "Afterwards we'd all pile into the welfare and drink with the opposition. They usually stayed on in those days. The bar used to open for the evening session at six and we'd play till about eight. For two hours or so, men would come out with their pints and stand round the boundary to watch. There was a concrete edge around the perimeter, and beyond that were the allotments. If the ball went over there, you almost always had to find a new one." Particularly, it would seem, towards the end of the summer when a worn red sphere could be completely hidden under the shadow of marrows the size of zeppelins and onions that could prick the tear ducts from twenty yards. Miners grew vegetables with the competitive edge that they brought to whippet-breeding and cricket.

Mike never worked down the pit. He was a clerk in the local Coal Board office when he started playing here in 1960, aged fifteen. Keeping wicket on the old Newstead Colliery pitch required a youthful athleticism. "Every pit had its own groundsman, supplied by the Coal Industry

Social Welfare Organisation (CISWO), and this one was hard and true," he recalls. "But we had some lively bowlers and there was a slight slope. Luckily, Howard Burrows preferred to bowl uphill from the welfare end. He was very tall and brought the ball down from well over nine feet."

The cricket was not quite so competitive by the 1980s, Mike maintains. But the colliery team was still producing useful players when closure came. Five or six of them joined Newstead Abbey and helped propel the club up the league. What was once Lord Byron's stately pile is just down the road from the former pit village and the grounds provide an idyllic backdrop for cricket. "It *is* lovely," Mike concedes, "particularly in early summer when the rhododendrons are out. But the pitch is too small for first-team cricket in this league and we can't do much about it — or rebuild the pavilion — because of the restrictions on a heritage site."

So while he and his second-team colleagues press on in this sylvan setting, the first team now plays on a new ground across the railway line from the old one where Dave Atkins caught fire and the Mike Murphy caught everything he could. In the absence of CISWO, it was laid down by the local borough council. "I think they wanted to put some life back into the area," Mike surmises as we pull up next to one of those mock winding wheels commemorating Newstead Colliery (1884-1987). He leaves the heater on. It's deep mid-winter and the pitch is currently hosting football. But we can see the covers in the shadow of a small firm making reinforced concrete and providing what looks like one of the few means of employment round here. "The setting's pretty bland," he sighs, "and the pitch is nowhere near as good as the old one. Anything we leave outside gets vandalised; even the heavy roller."

As we drive away, we can see across the wasteland of what were once the allotments to the ruin of what was once the miners' welfare. Somewhere in between, under the foundations of those soulless semis, lie the memories of a veteran wicket keeper and those who were once useful batsmen and fiery fast bowlers.

Stanford Hall

Nick Shaw is not difficult to spot outside Loughborough Station. The secretary of Wymeswold Cricket Club, six foot three in a sleeveless cricket sweater over a t-shirt, bears a marked resemblance to the comedian Harry Hill. He drives more like Damon Hill. But we arrive at Stanford Hall on the Nottinghamshire-Leicestershire border in one piece, sail through the gates and down the drive. "There it is," says Nick excitedly. Soon he's striding ahead, peering into the grass in search of something — anything — to indicate that this was once was the most fabled country-house cricket venue in the land. All we can see are a few straggly dandelions and some golden leaves bowling along in a mild autumnal breeze. A stout oak at deep square leg is one of an array of deciduous trees ranged around what used to be the boundary.

"We started playing here in the late '70s when our club was known as Rempstone," Nick goes on. "It was properly maintained then — a beautiful wicket and out-field." But its heyday had been fifty summers earlier when Sir Julien Cahn owned the Georgian hall and the 3,000 acres around it. Sir Julien made his fortune in the hire purchase furniture business. He was a philan-thropist as well as president and bankroller of Nottinghamshire CCC. What's more, he was prepared to pay for some of the world's finest cricketers to come and play Sunday matches on his doorstep. Not just to watch them, however. Cahn expected to play. Yet, as *The Cricketer* magazine observed in September, 1997, he was 'at once the most prolific patron of cricket between the wars and comfortably the worst-ever first-class cricketer.'

J.M. Barrie, who briefly worked as a journalist in Nottingham before going on to write *Peter Pan*, once observed that Sir Julien's deliveries were so slow that if he didn't like one he could run after it and fetch it back. But at least there was an element of surprise in the occasional ball from Cahn — the one that climbed so high that the batsman seemed to have forgotten that it was up there. How else do we explain his dismissal of Kumar Shri Duleepsinhji (Cambridge University, Sussex and England)? "Halfway through the ball's flight, Duleepsinhji seemed to lose interest and sat on the end of his bat handle awaiting a return from outer space," writes Cahn's biographer Miranda Rijks. "The look of consternation on his face when the ball landed on top of two trembling bails was a picture indeed."

Even more remarkable was Sir Julien's apparent hold over Frank Woolley of Kent and England, widely regarded as one of the most elegant left-handers of his or any other time. He trapped him on more than one occasion and would always bring himself on to bowl when Wooolley came in, muttering to his fellow members of the Sir Julien Cahn XI: "Here comes my rabbit."

Such triumphs with the ball were rare indeed for *The Eccentric Entrepreneur*, as Rijks dubbed him in the title of her biography. The six balls with which he took wickets in a career that spanned at least thirteen seasons (not to mention winter tours of the 'dominions' with his almost invincible XI) were mounted on silver plinths and displayed in the library at Stanford Hall.

Sir Julien was no better at other aspects of the game. He took evasive action if the ball came anywhere near him in the field and, when he went into bat, he took the precaution of donning inflatable pads. They were blown to a pressure of 23 lbs all round by Robson, chauffeur of his Rolls-Royce Phantom 2. 'Deliveries flew off the pads like a tennis ball thrown against a brick wall,' writes Duncan Hamilton in his biography of Harold Larwood, one of several Notts players whom the president supported financially and unofficially. 'But no umpire dared give a leg bye against Cahn when he was batting.'

Between 1926 and 1939, Sir Julien lavished between £20,000 and £30,000 a year on local cricket, transforming Trent Bridge in the process. He had another ground, West Park, laid out within ten minutes walk of the county headquarters and it was there that his XI took on touring teams from every country, apart from Australia, who would have been too big a draw for an occasion that was free to the public. It was in the elegant Lutyens-style pavilion at West Park that Sir Julien tried to persuade Larwood to sign an apology for the furore caused by the infamous bodyline tour of 1932-3. To his eternal credit, the great bowler declined. But why was Cahn doing the MCC's dirty work? Perhaps he was desperate to ingratiate himself with an organisation that looked down on him as a Jew who made his money through trade. Anti-Semitism was as rife as snobbery among the English upper classes in the 1930s.

The pavilion is still there, thanks to a campaign lead by Notts archivist and librarian Peter Wynne-Thomas which scuppered a scheme to build apartments on the site. The West Park pitch is still there too. It's now the headquarters of the West Bridgford British Legion team. They also played occasional games at Stanford Hall until around fifteen years ago when the days of this illustrious country house ground were already numbered. "It was a beautiful setting to play, but there was no changing room and no showers," recalls club secretary Chris Roper, who still stands behind the stumps at 53, either as umpire or wicket keeper. "After a game on a hot day, some of our lads dived in the swimming pool to cool off." That would be the same pool in which Lady Cahn, strapped for something to buy as a birthday present for the man who had everything, once installed a pair of sea lions.

Chris learnt much about Sir Julien from his father who played for the Legion before him. "And my Uncle Eric," he adds, "He told me about the boat full of women moored on the Trent when touring teams came to Nottingham." Idle talk? Well, possibly not. Rijks's biography mentions the women, if not the boat: 'Legend says that Sir Julien always provided 10 girls for the opposing teams after major games. When asked why he only provided 10, the answer came: "Because the chap who got me out didn't get a girl".' He also ensured that cricketing visitors to Stanford Hall were well wined and dined. Particularly the opposition. On those rare occasions when his XI had a bad morning, opposing players would be detained over port and cigars for a period that far exceeded the norm for a cricketing lunch break. His own side were expected to observe strict quotas until after stumps were drawn. That may, in part, help to explain why they lost only nineteen of the 621 games they played until the outbreak of war in 1939. The major factor, however, was the quality of players he could call upon. His team that toured Jamaica in 1929, for instance, included Wilfred 'Dodge' Whysall of Notts, Ewart Astill of Leicestershire, Andy Sandham of Surrey and Lord Tennyson of Hampshire, grandson of the poet. England players all.

Sir Julien died in 1944. The following year, house and grounds were sold for £54,000. To the Co-op, as it happens, which used the Georgian mansion as a training school and, in keeping with more egalitarian times, offered the cricket pitch to local clubs. The Co-op finally sold up at the end of the century and, in 2009, the property developer Chek Whyte was granted planning permission to build a £60 million luxury retirement village on the site – only to see his plans undermined by mounting debts which he blamed on the recession. The hall is still there, shrouded in memories of more colourful days.

The same could be said of what was once the cricket pitch where Nick Shaw, having unsuccessfully scoured the undergrowth for signs of where the wicket used to be, is reliving a few memories of his playing days with Rempstone before it evolved into Wymeswold. "I remember getting my highest score of 80-something here, including a late cut from which we ran five. It's a long boundary down there," he adds, pointing to a distant wall over which outhouses protrude, including some greenhouse roofs. The nursery end, you might say. "As secretary, the Co-op asked me to take out insurance in case somebody put a six through one of them," he goes on. "But I never did. We managed to hit it twice and they only billed us once — for 40 quid. Whenever someone bowled rubbish, though, we always called it a 'greenhouse ball'."

As we set off back down the drive, I can't help wondering what the glass bill must have been like when Sir Julien was tossing up greenhouse balls to some of the world's greatest batsmen.

Britain's Lost Cricket Grounds by Chris Arnot is published in October 2011 by Aurum Press, priced £25. The book covers the whole country, but here we print the introduction followed by two chapters from Nottinghamshire.

Graham Greene
In Nottingham
David Belbin

When Graham Greene arrived in Nottingham in November 1925, he was a new Oxford graduate, just turned 21, who wanted to get into journalism. He hoped that a brief spell as an unpaid trainee sub-editor on the *Nottingham Journal* would stand him in good stead for a post in London. On November 1st, 1925, he moved into lodgings on Hamilton Road in Forest Fields. The exact house number is unknown and the building itself is long gone.

'When I read Dickens on Victorian London,' he wrote in his 1971 autobiography, *A Sort Of Life*, 'I think of Nottingham in the twenties. There was an elderly 'boots' still employed at the Black Dog Inn, there were girls suffering from unemployment in the lace trade, who would, so it was said, sleep with you in return for a high tea with muffins, and a haggard blue-haired prostitute, ruined by amateur competition, haunted the corner by W.H. Smith's bookshop. Trams rattled downhill through the goose-market and on to the blackened castle. Against the rockface leant the oldest pub in England with all the grades of a social guide: the private bar, the saloon, the ladies', the snug, the public... I had found a town as haunting as Berkhamstead, (one) where years later I would lay the scene of a novel and of a play... it was the focal point of failure, a place undisturbed by ambition, a place to be resigned to, a home from home.'

Green visited many of the town's cinemas, where matinee seats in the stalls cost fourpence. He would watch movies back to back, deepening the relationship with the cinema that was to feed the film criticism and scripts he was to write in the next three decades. He spent so much time at the city's numerous cinemas because of the hours he worked at the *Nottingham Journal*: 5.30 to midnight, allowing him plenty of time for cheap matinees.

He didn't stay long in Hamilton Road, where the boarding house's other residents were two old ladies, with whom he played cards on his first night, and 'an awful man... whose mind is the lowest cesspool of dirt I've ever come across.' But he had trouble escaping. He told his landlady that he needed a room to himself. She promptly put her sitting room at his disposal, at no extra cost. He then told her that he wanted to bring over his dog, Paddy, from Berkhamstead. She said she loved dogs. He wrote to his fiancée:

'I can't very well explain that I don't like having meals at a table with other people, & that I intensely dislike some of her guests.'

His negative feelings about the city were probably affected by how much he missed his fiancée, Vivien. But he did find things to like.

'There's a most marvellous fog here today, my love. It makes walking a thrilling adventure. I've never been in such a fog before in my life. If I stretch out my walking stick in front of me, the ferrule is half lost in obscurity. Coming back, I twice lost my way, & ran into a cyclist, to our mutual surprise. Stepping off a pavement to cross to the other side becomes a wild and fantastic adventure... if you never hear from me again, you will know that I am moving round in little plaintive circles, looking for a pavement.'

Not long after writing this, in mid-November, he moved to new digs near the Arboretum, ten minutes walk from work, where he had his own room. In his autobiography he described it as 'a grim grey row with a grim grey name, Ivy House, All Saints Terrace.' Full board was 35 shillings a week and he had his own living room. 'My landlady was a thin complaining widow with a teenaged daughter, and when my future wife, Vivien, visited me for a holiday weekend, the girl let down a cotton-reel from

upstairs and banged it on my ground-floor window to dis-
turb our loving quiet... On overcast mornings, before
going on with my hopeless novel, I would take (Paddy) for
a walk in the nearby park where, when you touched the
leaves, they left soot on the fingers. Once I took a lace
worker to high tea, but she didn't sleep with me for all
that. Oxford seemed more than six months away and
London very far. I had fallen into a pocket out of life and
out of time, but I was not unhappy.'

The landlady, Mrs Loney, was evidently lazy. Her 'gentlemen clean their own shoes,' she told Greene. And she
was nosy. She lived in the basement of the house which
meant that she could not see across the street. One day
she asked Greene whether she could use his ground floor
window to observe a man down the way being taken to
hospital. Another time Greene came home to find her in
his room, writing a letter. She had a penchant for tinned
salmon and gave it Greene for tea most nights. He often
shared it with his dog, even though it meant that Paddy
would be sick on the floor.

All of the time that he was in Nottingham, Greene kept
returning to Vivien in London, where he chased up contacts who might give him a job on a London paper. He
also wrote to the *Yorkshire Post, Glasgow Herald* and
Manchester Guardian in search of paid work.

'The *Journal* prided itself on its literary tradition,' he
wrote. 'The paper might be considered vulgar but at least
it was bohemian. Sir James Barrie (author of *Peter Pan*)
had once been a member of staff, and there was even a
living novelist who had graduated on the *Journal* and
had a house in the town.' This was Cecil Roberts, now
best known for the room named after him in
Nottingham's City Library but, in his day, a prolific and
popular novelist. Roberts invited Greene to tea where 'he
told me that in the seven years since he had become independent of journalism he had saved enough to give him a
settled income of four hundred pounds a year... Perhaps
I looked at him with too great an envy — I could have

married on four hundred a year — for he hastened to tell me how perilous the future was. (He really was Mr Micawber in reverse.)' Greene gave him a copy of his slim pamphlet of verse, *Babbling April* and they talked for an hour, after which Greene wrote to Vivien 'an educated person in Nottingham is as precious & rare a find as jam in a wartime doughnut!'

Greene did meet one other educated person in Nottingham, one who had a huge effect on him. In order to marry Vivien, it was necessary for Greene, an atheist, to convert to Roman Catholicism. Soon after his arrival, he 'took Paddy for a walk to the sooty neo-Gothic Cathedral — it possessed for me a certain gloomy power because it represented the inconceivable and the incredible. There was a wooden box for enquiries and I dropped into it a note asking for instruction. I had no intention of being received into the church. For such a thing to happen I would need to be convinced of its truth and that was not even a remote possibility.'

He was given a tutor, Father Trollope, once a West End actor and himself a late convert. Greene didn't at first tell him that he wanted to marry a Catholic girl. Once or twice a week, he took instruction for an hour. In his autobiography he says he became convinced by Catholicism but has long since forgotten why he was convinced. Nevertheless, in his last month in the city, February, he was received into the church. In *A Sort Of Life* he writes that his first confession was 'a humiliating ordeal. Later we may become hardened to the formulas of confession and sceptical about ourselves... But in the first Confession a convert really believes in his promises. I carried mine down with me like heavy stones into an empty corner of the Cathedral, dark already in the early afternoon, and the only witness of my baptism was a woman who had been dusting the chairs. I took the name Thomas — after St Thomas the doubter and not Thomas Aquinas — and then I went on to the *Nottingham Journal* office and the football results and the evening of potato chips.' The Catholic novelist was born.

Greene lived in Nottingham for only four months, a period he shortens by a month in his autobiography. He left without a job to go to, and wrote to Vivien from London: 'Thank God, Nottingham is over. It's like coming back into real life again, being here.' Ten days later, he got a job on the *Times*, a job he wouldn't have got without his experience on the *Nottingham Journal*.

'Four months is quite a large slice of existence,' he wrote to Vivien. And for him, this turned out to be true. Greene set one of his best early novels, *A Gun For Sale* in Nottingham, lightly fictionalised as Nottwich, as well as his play *The Potting Shed*. Nottwich is also referred to in his fine 1958 novel *Our Man in Havana*. Versions of Ivy House and Mrs Loney appear in several novels. Although he later talked about the city affectionately, this was rarely his attitude in the letters to Vivien. 'This town makes one want a mental and physical bath every quarter of an hour,' he wrote. 'There's absolutely nothing worth doing in this place. No excitement, no interest, nothing worth a halfpenny curse.' Yet the city was important — many argue, crucially important — to his fiction, presenting him with a first hand experience of the working class that may have prevented him from becoming just another chronicler of upper middle class life in London.

A fuller account of Greene's period in Nottingham can be found in chapters 17–18 of the first volume of Norman Sherry's three volume official biography, to which I am indebted. Sherry is inaccurate in just one regard. He includes a photo of the second boarding house where Greene stayed, but it does not show the building he refers to in the text, one that most Greene scholars consider to be 'Ivy House', which is pictured overleaf. Number 2, All Saints Terrace, is a multi-occupation house on a slightly tricky to find corner equidistant from Forest Road West and Waverley Street. It is near the Arboretum, a short walk from the city centre.

A few years ago I showed number two to David Lodge, a Catholic novelist and great admirer of Greene, when he came to give a Graham Greene memorial lecture. David wrote about his visit in a diary piece for the *New Statesman*. 'There is no plaque' he concluded. The absence of a plaque is probably to the good. I have since discovered that I didn't just take him to the wrong house. I took him to the wrong street.

Recently, when I was asked to write an earlier version of this essay by Nottingham Playhouse, I came across a blog piece by Andrew Schlich and Jim Thornton. These Nottingham Greene fans had a new theory about where the author lived during his brief spell in the city. It couldn't be 2, All Saints Terrace, they argued, because Number 2 has no room for a basement flat, which doesn't fit with Greene's account of his landlady living in one. Furthermore, they argued that the current All Saints Terrace wasn't so named in the 1920s and that what Greene referred to as All Saints Terrace was the back of All Saints Road. This road used not to have a name, but is now called Goodwin Street. The two lines of houses

that back on to Goodwin Street fit Greene's description in his one Nottingham novel, *A Gun For Sale*, where he writes of 'two rows of small neo-Gothic houses lined up as carefully as a company on parade'.

In 2010 I went for a walk along Goodwin Street and environs with Andrew Schlich, who works in the area, and screenwriter Michael Eaton, an avid Greene fan, who lives nearby. The big, multi-occupied houses that back onto Goodwin Street have the requisite basement rooms where the landlady might have lived. Also, Greene would have needed to climb some stairs to get to his ground floor bedsit, as his letters suggest, and that fits too. We were convinced.

Short of getting hold of all the property deeds for the houses on All Saints Road and Goodwin Street and happening upon the names of Mrs Loney or 'Ivy House', there seems little chance of establishing which particular building used to be Greene's lodgings. Andrew would like to see a blue plaque on the end of the street anyway. Good luck to that. Some would argue that Greene was in Nottingham for such a short time, and was so rude about it, he's lucky to have even one memorial in the city. For there is already a plaque recalling Greene the journalist in the Watson Fothergill building that used to house the *Nottingham Journal and News* offices on Upper Parliament Street. Given that he wrote about how little he learnt there (and complained that he was forced to draw an allowance from his headmaster father 'who could ill afford it') even this plaque might seem rather generous.

In London, Greene ditched the dog and moved to Battersea. He worked from four to eleven at the *Times* for five pounds a week. The novel he was writing in Nottingham was never published. Nor was the one after. It would be 1928 before Heinemann accepted his third attempt, *The Man Within*, which appeared the following year. But his recollections of and relationship with Nottingham never left him. In time, they would be transmogrified into one of the seedier sections in a new territory, one that would come to be known as Greeneland.

Welcome to the New Hull
Ross Bradshaw

'Welcome to the New Hull' says the hoarding at the train station. What can it mean? 'We now have arcades with the same shops that you have at home, even Greggs'? 'Hull Gay Pride is on July 31st'? The hoarding is silent on detail.

Still, the cafe where I drafted this article has wifi, and a warm croissant, fresh orange juice and excellent coffee came to £3.60. My Hull friends say that Hull people do like a bargain. Philip Larkin's famous poem about the city, 'Here' referred to the 'cut price crowd'. My B & B cost me £24, and a haircut set me back £7, so he was right.

Actually it is the old Hull I wanted to see. The Wilberforce House and Museum to begin with (though I hope that when Desmond Tutu dropped by he was not on his own, as I was), which also contains a small but fascinating exhibition on Larkin. The Museum is nicely laid out, though the material was familiar. Seems a strange place to put the Larkin exhibition though. The material there too was familiar, from what we know of Larkin. His personal books were there, jazz records, stuff from his domestic life, but there is also mention of his rather unusual love life and his interest in the seamy side. No sensationalism though.

This year was 'Larkin 25', and Hull had a year-round Festival marking it. Most people will know he was the local university librarian, and many will also know that Hull became a centre of British poetry, with so many well known poets — Sean O'Brien, Roger McGough, Douglas Dunn and more — passing through. Unusually for birds of passage, the Hull years stayed important in their lives, marking them permanently. Maybe it is the feeling of being at the end of the line. Maybe it is the cream telephone boxes. Maybe it is the number of tattoo parlours... Hull is a port city and it shows. At one time there were special railway station platforms for migrants, and, in the old town there is a plaque marking the Harry Lazarus Hotel, a way station for those bound for elsewhere. I stayed in the Spring Bank area which has Kurdish and Polish shops, as well as cafes for supporters of Hull Kingston Rovers. Hull wears its multiculturalism easily, it seems to me.

I wanted to find the spot on the River Hull where James Booth from the Philip Larkin Society took the photograph gracing the cover of Five Leaves' *Old City, New Rumours*, an anthology of Hull poets. I wandered about until I found the spot, in fact just behind the Wilberforce House where I'd been three hours earlier, just down from the old deserted harbour. Then I looked for the street called The Land of Green Ginger, the best street name in the world, which will be known to many readers as the title of a book by Winifred Holtby. But I forgot to search for the famous tiny window in the street.

One part of the 'New Hull' I was pleased to see was the headquarters of the Hull Truck theatre company, a large and friendly arts centre. Humber Mouth Book Festival had organised a reading by Andrew Motion, linked to *Old City, New Rumours*, so it seemed a good time to visit. The tickets described him as the ex-Poet Laureate, while 'former' seems kinder, but he did seem to have been liberated by leaving the laureateship behind him. Various other Hull poets were in the audience, but I was unable to meet Maurice Rutherford, who would shortly have a new poetry collection out from Nottingham's Shoestring Press. Maurice, more than any other poet, talks with Larkin in his own poems. He is the 'son of a Hull fish curer's manager/and writer of occasional short verse' whose earlier slim volume of poems was credited in Hull library to the more famous Margaret. Maurice, a grand letter writer in the old tradition, is still being published in his 90s and knew those 'head-scarved wives', 'grim' and otherwise, that Larkin observed.

Returning home, I discussed the city with a few former residents. One remarked that the place always did contain an inordinate number of people with tattoos; a second wanted to talk only of his time in nearby Grimsby, claiming still to carry the emotional scars. The third, Roy Lang, who sadly died recently, had been a contemporary of Maureen Lipman in the Hull Jewish community. He loved living there. He talked of often coming home to find his father, a natural linguist whose firm sold clothing to visiting sailors, in foreign conversation at the kitchen table with a ship's captain from Iceland or one of many countries whose boats brought trade to the area. Roy laughed and laughed at the thought that I'd liked his hometown and called in his wife – who is from the opposite coast – so she could hear directly that a visitor had taken a shine to the place he looked back on with such affection.

***

Ian Parks, a productive ex-Hull poet, sent me the poem overleaf, written late the same night, which seems to capture the city well.

The Land of Green Ginger
Ian Parks

Here is the smallest window
in the world. Look through it
squinting with one eye.
You'll see the things
you're not supposed to see:
the politician cheating

on his wife, the fat priest
stealing from the poor,
the poet scribbling
someone else's lines.
Only in this quarter,
in this district of the town

and only through this green
and stamp-sized frame
that didn't shatter in the blitz
can you expect to see
things as they really are.

Other windows hide from us,

distract us and distort.
But this is the Land
of Green Ginger —
a place where the sky
and the estuary meet;
where all the thin alleys

deceive, double-back
and lead to a spot
where strangeness occurs.
Put your eye to the window,
see how England goes:
its coalitions and its wars,

the steady consolation
of the rain, the failure
to respond or change
its constitution or its laws.
Once I drank bitter
from a clouded glass

among the city's dissident
and peered out later
on the green-tinged street
where the world of trade
and commerce came and went,
their ebb and flow

refracted and contained
inside the confines
of a thick glass pane.
The barmaid blinked
a tear back from her eye.
Then, after drinking

I went out into the bright
unequivocal day,
arrived too early or too late.
For this is the Land
of Green Ginger
and this is the window

that never lies —
where looking just once
means looking again
at what you think you know
in this city of lost chances
where the rail-lines terminate.

Writing in the Snow:
or translating what
you don't understand
Andy Croft

What is translation? On a platter
A poet's pale and glaring head,
A parrot's screech, a monkey's chatter,
And profanation of the dead.

(Vladimir Nabokov, 'On Translating Eugene Onegin')

Nabokov of course famously refused to translate Pushkin's *Evgeny Onyegin* into verse, relying instead on what he called his 'honest roadside prose'. His argument was partly about metre and partly about the relative paucity of rhyme in English. But it was mostly about the ownership of cultural knowledge:

> *Anyone who wishes to attempt a translation of* Onegin *should acquire exact information in regard to a number of relevant subjects, such as the Fables of Krilov, Byron's works, French poets of the eighteen century, Rousseau's* La Nouvelle Héloïse, *Pushkin's biography, banking games, Russian songs relating to divination, Russian military ranks of the time as compared to Western European and American ones, the difference between cranberry and lingenberry, the rules of the English pistol duel as used in Russia, and the Russian language...*

It is an intimidating list (lingenberries?), in which the ability to speak the language appears to be the last requirement for the translator. Few people are equally at home in more than one culture, whatever their grasp of languages (and Nabokov's facility with the English language did not inoculate him against the charms of William F. Buckley and Richard Nixon). This is the school of translation that says you have to know a culture before you can understand it, that can render the meaning but not the sense of a text, the reason but not the rhyme. Although the result may be fine scholarship (Nabokov's 'footnotes reaching up like skyscrapers') it isn't always poetry.

But there are, of course, other ways of translating, other ways of making sense of the world. Sometimes *not* understanding — even *mis*understanding — can be a virtue. Too much luggage can slow the traveller down.

A few years ago I found myself in Siberia for two weeks without any luggage at all. My bag clearly preferred the idea of a quick break in sunny Tashkent to Siberia in winter. Having to wash the same clothes every night for two weeks was a bit wearing, although thanks to Siberian central heating my clothes were always cardboard crisp the next morning. More frustrating was the fact that my missing bag contained all the copies of the book I was supposed to be launching. Although we had good audiences at readings in Novosibirsk and Kemerovo, without any books to sell, sales were not good. 'Exclusively available in Tashkent' is not a great sales pitch when you are in Siberia.

Book launches? Siberia? What about the howling of the wolves, the salt-mines, the Gulags and sub-zero temperatures? Siberia has of course always been linked in the British imagination with violent and wintry extremes. Rasputin was born in Siberia. Lenin was exiled there. Mandelshtam died there. Maxim Gorky called it 'a land of chains and ice'. But Siberia is also home to forty million people. It is the place where European Russia meets Asia head-on, a land of extreme natural beauty that crosses seven time zones. Novosibirsk is Russia's third largest city, an industrial centre which boasts the largest opera house in Russia. Kemerovo — the industrial capital of the Kuzbass — was built in the early 1920s by Communists from the USA, Canada and Britain, invited by Lenin to help build the Revolution. Siberia is a spectacular

44

concentration of Russia's virtues and its vices — bureaucracy, generosity, inefficiency and spontaneous kindness. Cold weather, warm people. There is more to life in Siberia than ice-princesses, shamans and dodgy oligarchs. And more to Russian poetry than Moscow and St Petersburg.

I first visited Siberia in 2004, as part of the Arts Council/British Council 'Reading across the Lines' project (which also included the poets Bill Herbert and Paul Summers). Since then I have worked with the British Council in Novosibirsk and at the University of Kemerovo. Meetings with poets and translators in Siberia led to the idea of a selection of contemporary poets from Siberia. This was eventually published in 2007 by Smokestack Books, as *Permanent Winter,* with a series of launch readings in the UK and in Siberia.

In Spring 2008, Bill, Paul and I spent ten days in Moscow, writing a book of poems about the Moscow Metro, a commitment we had made to ourselves when we first visited the city several years earlier. After the London Underground and the Newcastle Metro, the Moscow system was — well, we didn't know how to put it into words. How do you translate a stunned, confused and humbled silence?

The Moscow Metro is one of the busiest underground railway networks in the world. Every year over 2.5 billion passengers travel its 300 km of track between its 177 stations. But it is also an extraordinary museum, a people's palace and a dazzling art gallery. It is a place where engineering, science and function meet art, architecture and ideology. The stations are named after great events in Russian history, and Russia's greatest writers, artists and scientists. The Metro is celebrated in poetry and popular song, film and fiction, by writers from Mayakovsky and Brecht to Lukyanenko. When the poet Dmitri Prigov died in 2007, friends and admirers held a banquet in his memory on a Circle Line train.

The Metro is also a kind of cross-section of Russian history, an infernal map of the purgatorial circles through which the country has passed. In 1941, with the German army outside Moscow, Stalin addressed a mass meeting to mark the anniversary of the October Revolution on the platforms of Mayakovskaya station. In the Great Patriotic War the stations were used as bomb shelters; during the Cold War they were designated as nuclear shelters. Today they are a place of warmth and shelter for the city's dogs and drunks.

The resulting book — *Three Men on the Metro* — was published by Five Leaves in 2009. It consists of ninety poems and prose pieces, songs and sonnets (almost half of the book is written in the sonnet form used by Pushkin in *Onyegin*), postcard poems, found poems, snap-shots, diary entries and music downloads. The core of the book is a series of poems about individual stations — notably Borovitskaya, Tsaristino, Kitai-Gorod, Kievskaya, Prospekt Mira, Taganskaya, Chkalovskaya, Rimskaya, Mendeleevskaya, VDNKh, Oktyabrskaya, Stretenskiy Bul'var, Mayakovskaya, Partisanskaya and Komsomol-skaya. And there are poems about hitting the tourist-trail — we were in Revolution Square on May Day, we went to a game of football (Lokomotiv v Spartak Nalchik), attended celebrations for the Orthodox Easter, visited a *banya* and took a boat trip on the Moscow River. We visited the Metro Museum, the Bulgakov Museum, the Patriarch Ponds, Tsaritsino Park, Red Square, the VDNK Park, the Vernissage, the Gagarin Monument and the Sparrow Hills.

For we were tourists in a strange city, hopelessly out of our depth, often lost, unable to speak very much Russian and relying on out-of-date guide-books. *Three Men on the Metro* is not so much a book about Moscow as about being a tourist in Moscow. It is a study in being bewildered and overwhelmed by a culture which we could not possibly understand. Our guide in this (hence the book's title) was Jerome K. Jerome's *Three Men on a Boat* (a cult classic in the Soviet Union). Accordingly, we took as one of the book's epigraphs a line from Jerome's *Three Men on the Bummel* — 'There will be no useful information in this book'. It is a way of admitting how little we understood, how much is always lost in translation.

Although the book was, of course, almost completely ignored by the British poetry scene, a Russian edition of the book is in preparation by Paulsen/Novoye Izdatel'stvo. A Russian translation of our attempts to 'translate' Russian culture — what would Nabokov have thought? But the world does not always make as much sense as we might wish. The Outsider can sometimes recognise what the Insider can no longer see. Trying to understand another language can be like trying to learn how to read a different kind of weather:

This sky's a foreign language
  Whose native speakers know
It takes the earth's thesaurus
  To catch the falling snow.
As well as try translating
  The way the weather talks —
In Russian verbs of motion
  Snow doesn't fall, it *walks*.
It ambles, shambles, gambols,
  It sidles, idles, creeps,
It bounces, pounces, flounces,
  It pirouettes and leaps,
It does the hokey-cokey,
  The twist, the cha-cha-cha
In a silent karaoke
  In Snegurochka's Bar.

Small children play at statues
  Outside the ice-carved shops
Till everybody freezes,
  And when the music stops
The speechless world is deafened
  By the ringing in our ears
Like underwater singing
  Or the music of the spheres.

The sound of snowflakes walking
  Through Kemerovo at night
Would silence anyone who doubts
  That happiness writes white,
The colour of the senses
  At ten degrees below,
Where no matter what the question,
  The answer's always snow.

In my terrible, plodding, childish Russian I frequently confuse the word 'pi*satel*' (someone who writes) with '*pis*atel' (someone who pisses). This can be embarrassing. But in Siberia in winter it is perfectly possible to do both at the same time.

Mapping Gissing's
Workers in the Dawn
Richard Dennis

Making maps of novels has a long tradition. Some stories, such as *Treasure Island*, come with their own maps. Closer to Gissing's London, Arthur Morrison's *Child of the Jago* (1896) featured a frontispiece map of the 'Jago,' plotting out a street pattern almost identical to that of the real 'Nichol' in Shoreditch, but substituting Morrison's names: the real 'Mead Street' became 'Honey Lane', 'Boundary Street' became 'Edge Lane', and so forth. Other novels received maps courtesy of their publishers — OUP's 'A Map of Mrs Dalloway's London' and Penguin's 'Central London in the Mid-Twenties' are just simplified street maps of 1920s London to help readers unfamiliar with the metropolis to follow the routes of characters in *Mrs Dalloway* as they weave their way across the West End.[1] Blackwell's map of 'The London of Mrs Dalloway' is annotated with numbered references to incidents in the text. But none of these maps plot the characters' walks. They merely mark locations that would allow readers to construct their own geographies of the novel.[2]

At the other analytical extreme are Franco Moretti's maps of novels by Dickens, Balzac, Flaubert, and Conan Doyle, some simply marking the locations of key events or characters' homes, but others more abstractly identifying clusters of characters in topographical and social space to produce Venn diagrams of overlapping or interpenetrating social worlds superimposed on maps of London and Paris, or charting, in the case of *Our Mutual Friend*, the movement of the narrative from one part of the city to another through successive monthly instalments.[3] As important are the blank spaces that emerge and the

49

divides that are rarely crossed. In this way, Moretti makes the argument for the evolution of Dickens's London from a simple bi-polar poor east and comfortable west in *Oliver Twist* to a more complex social geography by the time of *Our Mutual Friend*, especially involving the emergence of what Moretti terms a 'third London.'[4]

The relevance of using maps not simply to record locations mentioned in texts but as analytical tools connecting the structure of novels to the structure of the cities in which they are set should be self-evident to Gissing scholars. Gissing's London locations are usually real places, often precisely designated and drawn from his own experience; but more than this, they are selected with a purpose: not simply containers for the narrative but characters in their own right. Even in *Isabel Clarendon* (1886), not normally thought of as a London novel, and mainly set in imaginary rural environments, Gissing is very precise in his choice of London locations — 'that desolate region through which stagnates the Regent's Canal, the north end of Camden Town'; followed by rooms 'in Highgate, not far from the pleasant road which leads across the valley to Hampstead; four rooms and an underground kitchen'; immediately contrasted with the Meres's house in Chelsea: 'a small house in a little square, between which and the river is a portion of Cheyne Walk. Three minutes' walk brings you to the Albert Bridge...'; and Gabriel's home and studio 'on the north side of Regent's Park' looking west to 'the smug, plebeian slope of Primrose Hill.'[5] The role played by location is also very apparent in *The Unclassed*, in which Gissing changed some locations from the first edition (1884) when he revised the book a decade later. Slums in Westminster (1884) are shifted to the East End (1895), Pimlico becomes Fulham, Fulham becomes Tottenham. As I have argued elsewhere, we can speculate on why Gissing made these changes — the East End was certainly more in the public eye in 1895 than it had been a decade earlier, and Westminster had been 'improved' by

slum clearance, yet the novel remains set in the 1870s —
but the effect is to change the spatial dynamics of the
story, making for a more expansive, less constricted
metropolis, where characters had to make more use of
cabs and buses and coincidences in time and space might
be thought less likely. Geographically, therefore, the
novel is less 'naturally' realistic in its revised version.
Moreover, the meanings of some actions are changed:
Slimy drinking himself to death in Limehouse seems less
deliberate when he has only made the excursion from
somewhere else in the East End than when he has travelled all the way from Westminster; but Harriet is not so
early exposed as a liar when she tells her employer-cum-
landlady that she is off to see a friend in Westminster,
which is true in the first edition but false in the revised
edition.[6]

Placing *Workers*

The publication of a new edition of *Workers in the Dawn*
(1880), Gissing's sprawling, Dickensian first novel, offers
further scope for mapping, not only as a way of providing
readers with the whereabouts of long lost locations, such
as Adam & Eve Court, Little St Andrew Street, Crown
Street and the Debtors' Prison, but also as a tool for
exploring how Gissing sets space to work in his story.[7]
However, faced with less than perfect topographical
information, mapping is an imprecise art. Like complet-
ing Mahler's tenth or Elgar's third symphonies, the
mapmaker has to be granted some creative licence!

Some locations can be matched to the author's own experience: Gissing lived on Gower Place and Huntley Street
shortly before writing *Workers*, so it seems reasonable to
locate the lodgings occupied by Arthur Golding and Carrie,
the girl he disastrously marries, roughly where their cre-
ator lived. Charlotte Place, the home and workplace of the
radical printseller, Samuel Tollady, is such a short alley

between Goodge Street and Rathbone Place that at any but the most detailed scale you can't put the dot in the wrong place! But Portland Place, where the society painter, Gresham, had his home, is a longer street, and there are few clues as to where on the street he might have lived. Fortunately, it hardly matters, since this was a street of consistently high-class property. Suburban locations towards the end of the novel are also represented economically in the text — no more than the place-names, Islington, Highbury, Hampstead and Highgate. The greatest problem is where to locate the 'East End' in which the respectable artisan, Venning, and his daughter, Lucy, lived and where the nonconformist clergyman, Mr Heatherley, had his chapel, which accommodates a night school for girls (like Lucy), run by the earnest but sickly Helen Norman, Mr Gresham's ward, who is the real love of Arthur's life.

It is evident, both in the novel and in other contemporary writing, that the 'East End' was not as far east as we think of it today — Gissing alludes to the perception of West-Enders that Whitecross Street was 'very far off in that shocking East End which it is quite improper to think of, let alone visit.'[8] The only East End reference in his extant correspondence from pre-diary times (in his letter to his sister, Ellen, in February 1883) implies a location farther east of his usual travels — more like Whitechapel than Clerkenwell or Hoxton, but also suggests that he had not spent much time that far east before 1883.[9] Fortunately, there are at least two clues in the text of *Workers*. Helen commutes by train from Portland Place to her school in Heatherley's chapel, which implies she must have travelled by underground from Portland Road station (now Great Portland Street) east around what is now the Circle Line. Except that in 1870 when this part of the novel was set, the Metropolitan Railway extended only as far as Moorgate Street (today's Moorgate). From the station (not specified, but in 'The City'), 'It was not a very long walk to the chapel.'[10] Gissing was an avid walker but presumably he was mindful that this was not a long walk *for Helen*, so we might surmise that the chapel was no more than a few minutes' walk from Farringdon Road, Aldersgate Street (now Barbican) or Moorgate Street stations, probably the latter. Mr Heatherley's own home seems to have been in the opposite direction from the station, since it was not out of his way to accompany Helen back to the station at the end of her evening's classes, a walk which also took them past the Vennings' home. We also learn of Mr Heatherley that he lived 'in a street a short distance from the City Road,' although evidently not so directly connected to the main street for Helen not to have 'some little difficulty discovering the address.'[11] So we have a sequence of locations: Mr Heatherley's home — 'The City' station — the Vennings' home — the chapel; all within a few minutes' walk.

Only a few streets away from Moorgate Station was South Place Chapel, since 1824 the home of the South Place Religious Society, a dissenting congregation that had already abandoned belief in hell and the doctrine of the Trinity and was well on the way from unitarianism to humanism. In 1888 their abandonment of belief in God was signified by a change of name to the South Place Ethical Society and in the late 1920s the society moved to its present home, Conway Hall (named after its American minister from 1864 to 1885 and again from 1892 to 1897, Moncure Daniel Conway) in Red Lion Square, Holborn.[12] In February 1879, Gissing attended a lecture by G.W. Foote, editor of *The Liberal*, on 'Religion without a God,' held at 'South-place Institute.'[13] In contrast to South Place thinking, Mr Heatherley holds to conventional Christian doctrine, but unlike the Rev. Orlando Whiffle, Mrs Cumberbatch, or the unnamed Church of England clergyman to whom Helen first offers her services, he is not treated to Gissing's scorn. Indeed, when Helen quizzes Heatherley on his beliefs, the latter admits that 'the doctrine of eternal punishment has no

53

place in my creed.'[14] To this extent, at least, he shares the beliefs of the South Place society.

At the very least, I conclude, Gissing's visit to South Place played some part in situating Mr Heatherley, the Vennings and their chapel, in the vicinity of Moorgate and City Road, probably in Finsbury, to the north and east of Moorgate-City Road.

It is *possible*, of course, that their 'East End' lay *west* of City Road, which would return us to the vicinity of Whitecross Street; and the description of courts and alleys which Heatherley shows to Helen is not so different from what Gissing has already described in the case of Adam & Eve Court, or was later to describe in the case of 'Shooter's Gardens' in *The Nether World*, set in Clerkenwell. On the other hand, we might then have expected Gissing to allude to the proximity to Whitecross Street. The Vennings' own home is clearly *not* a slum, befitting Mr Venning's artisanal status, but we know from Charles Booth's survey at the end of the 1880s how close the 'semi-criminal' (coloured black on Booth's map) resided to the 'mixed' and the 'comfortable' (coloured purple and pink).[15]

In general, the more geographically central the location, the more precisely Gissing delineated it. Apart from the homes of characters, numerous specific West End locations mentioned in the novel include Grafton Street and Crown Street (both roughly on the line of the current Charing Cross Road, a street improvement completed in 1887), Leicester Square, Soho Square and Torrington Square, the Middlesex Hospital, the British Museum, the National Gallery, the Prince of Wales Theatre (in Tottenham Street), the Alhambra (Leicester Square) and the Oxford Music Hall (corner of Oxford Street and Tottenham Court Road) (where, much later, Gissing either accompanied or picked up his second wife, despite having roundly condemned it in *Workers* as no place for respectable young ladies, certainly not on their own).[16] Working our way towards the City, there are also references to Gray's Inn Square, Saffron Hill (of which, more below) and Paternoster Row. Less central, but quite specific locations include St Marylebone Workhouse, which Arthur passed on his way from Chapel Street (Edgware Road) (two more locations which figured prominently in Gissing's *later* life), the reservoir on Pentonville Road (Claremont Square, constructed as an open reservoir in the 1820s, covered over in 1852, but still functioning as a reservoir today), and Rotten Row, where Maud Gresham went riding, in Hyde Park. But more suburban locations — Arthur and Carrie's successive lodgings in Hampstead, Highgate and Camden Town, and Helen's home in 'Holly Cottage,' Highbury — are less easily reduced to points on a map. Arthur strayed as far as London Bridge, but the only character recorded as crossing the Thames to south London was Helen who, after surveying the 'mean and poverty-stricken' districts of Soho, Seven Dials, Drury Lane and Clare Market, extended her exploration 'through all the unutterable vileness which is to be found on the other side of the river, then through everything most heart-breaking that the wide extent of the East End has to show,' comments that indicate both their author's hazy knowledge of these parts of London and that the East End encompassed everywhere east of Clare Market, including both Saffron Hill and Clerkenwell.[17]

The most remote London location to be given a more precise setting was the church attended by Mrs Cumberbatch at the extremity of Mile End Road (presumably, somewhere east of the Regent's Canal): an outlandish location for an outlandish church (the Semi-United Presbyterio-Episcopal Church!), far beyond even the 'Oriental regions' of the near East End that Mr Gresham so frequently denigrates.[18] Another unmappable location is the whereabouts of another outlandish church, 'St Abinadab's,' an 'aristocratic church' where Mr Whiffle became incumbent, evidently somewhere in the fashionable West End since Helen is visited by fund-raising members of the congregation while she is living at

Portland Place and the Waghorns attend the church while they live in the vicinity of Regent's Park.[19]

In summary, it seems that Gissing's way of conceptualising the metropolis is a kind of map projection that exaggerates the area between the river and Euston Road, and between the West End and the City, but marginalises everywhere beyond those limits, a nineteenth-century equivalent to the famous London Underground map designed by Harry Beck in 1933, in which east and south-east London hardly exist at all, and the distance between middle-class suburbs (especially to the north-west) and the centre seems no greater than one side of the Circle Line to the other.[20]

Journeys: 1: Arthur's successive homes

There are also two kinds of journeys that seem to me to be worth mapping — the individual journeys on which Gissing sent his characters at key points in the novel, and their lifetime trajectories. I will begin by focusing on Arthur's, and the novel's, trajectory, which starts in Adam & Eve Court, a slum court opening off Whitecross Street. If Adam & Eve Court had not existed, it would have been reasonable enough for Gissing to have invented it: Adam & Eve is obviously an appropriate couple with which to begin an epic story, especially one concerned with growing up, good and evil, temptation, and the acquisition of (self)-knowledge. More presciently, Adam & Eve Court was an appropriate starting point for a lifelong career in storytelling. But, remarkably, Gissing did not need to invent it. The court was one of several on either side of Whitecross Street that were scheduled for demolition in 1877 under the terms of the 1875 Cross Act.

The Cross Act, steered through parliament by Disraeli's Home Secretary, Richard Cross, granted powers to local authorities (such as the Metropolitan Board of Works in

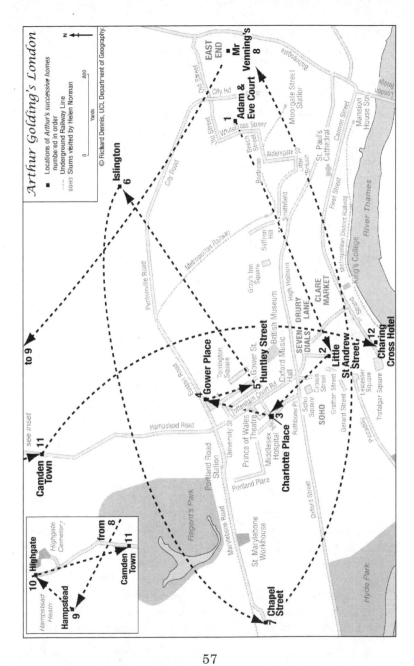

Arthur Golding's London

- ■ Locations of *Arthur's* successive homes numbered in order
- ---- Underground Railway Line
- SOHO Slums visited by Helen Norman

© Richard Dennis, UCL Department of Geography.

N

0   800
Yards

EAST END

Mr Venning's 8

Adam & Eve Court 1
Whitecross Street

City Rd

Old Street

Bath Street

Beech Street

Aldersgate St.

Barbican

Moorgate Street Station

Bishopsgate

St. Paul's Cathedral

Cannon Street

Mansion House Stn

London Bridge

River Thames

City Road

Metropolitan Railway

Pentonville Road

Islington 6

to 9

Gray's Inn Square

Smithfield

Saffron Hill

Little Britain

Fleet Street

King's College

Metropolitan District Railway

Holborn St.

High Holborn

CLARE MARKET

SEVEN DIALS

DRURY LANE

Little St Andrew Street 2

Charing Cross Hotel 12

Gower Place 4

Huntley Street 5

Gower St.

Torrington Square

British Museum

Oxford Music Hall

Tottenham Court Rd

Crown Street

Rathbone Pl.

SOHO

Grafton Street

Gerard Street

Leicester Square

Trafalgar Square

Piccadilly

Charlotte Place 3

Prince of Wales Theatre

Middlesex Hospital

University St.

Euston Road

Euston Road

Hampstead Road

Portland Road Station

Portland Place

Regent's Park

Marylebone Road

St Marylebone Workhouse

Hyde Park

Camden Town 11

see inset

Chapel Street 7

Highgate 10
Highgate Cemetery

Hampstead Heath

Hampstead 9

Camden Town 11

from 8

57

London) to compulsorily purchase and clear *areas* (as opposed to individual properties) designated as unfit for human habitation. The local authority was required to pay compensation at market values (i.e. what the land was worth when the slum had been cleared away, which was generally substantially more than under its current use), and to arrange for housing on the same site to accommodate as many persons as had been displaced, assuming occupancy levels of two persons per room. The local authority was not permitted to retain ownership of the site or the housing erected on it so, in practice, cleared sites were offered to private housing agencies — usually philanthropic trusts, like Peabody, or limited-dividend housing companies, like the Improved Industrial Dwellings Company — that were willing to meet the rehousing obligations. Given that the sites had previously been occupied by densely packed, insanitary dwellings, usually two or three storeys in height, the only way that redevelopment could provide sanitary accommodation for as many people as had lived there before was by building upwards, typically five- or six-storey 'block dwellings.' The terms of compensation, and the inability of philanthropic agencies to pay market rates for centrally located sites for working-class housing, invariably meant a substantial subsidy on the part of the local authority employing the legislation. This made it imperative that the boundaries of the 'slums' were drawn as tightly as possible, especially avoiding any commercial properties, such as breweries or small workshops where the loss of business and 'goodwill' entailed extra compensation.[21]

In the case of Whitecross Street the Medical Officer of Health for St Luke's proposed the clearance of areas in the district in official representations in November 1875 and November 1876, a local inquiry was held in April 1877, and a slightly reduced clearance area was confirmed by act of parliament on 23rd July 1877. Officially, 3,687 persons were to be displaced, although the real number was probably substantially higher. Clearance proceeded in sections, starting with the *west* side of Whitecross Street, which was cleared during 1880. The rest of the site, including Adam & Eve Court on the east side of Whitecross Street, was cleared in 1881. New streets, including what is now Dufferin Street, which runs along the south side of the line of Adam & Eve Court, were laid out in 1883. In total, the Metropolitan Board of Works spent £391,303 in purchasing land, clearing the site and laying out new streets, and received in return £76,360 (including £36,782 from the Peabody Donation Fund). The Peabody Trust took possession of the first area to be cleared (i.e. to the west) in December 1880, and of the remainder during 1881 and 1882. By April 1883, Peabody had completed six blocks of dwellings; and they reported that a grand total of 33 blocks of dwellings were occupied by January 1884.[22]

We can conclude, therefore, that Adam & Eve Court was still in existence when *Workers in the Dawn* was published, but that it was cleared, probably about a year after the book appeared, and was redeveloped as Peabody Buildings by the end of 1883.

This still does not tell us *how* familiar Gissing was with the real Adam & Eve Court. The *Times* (17th, 23rd, 26th April 1877) carried lengthy reports of the inquiry that preceded implementation of the scheme. Other newspapers featured briefer reports, and *The Standard* ran several articles on 'London Courts and Alleys,' including one (2nd Sept. 1875) devoted exclusively to Golden Lane, the street immediately west of Whitecross Street and also affected by the clearance scheme.[23] However, none of these reports singled out Adam & Eve Court and, in any case, they all predated Gissing's arrival in London in October 1877. I have not (yet) tracked down any newspaper articles naming the court, so Gissing must have discovered it for himself, perhaps through his reading of the 'Books on London Streets' listed on page 32 of his 'American Notebook,' or in the course of his exploration of 'the holes of London' alluded to in a letter from his brother, William, in June 1878.[24] William's anxiety — 'It must be very interesting examining the holes of London, as long as you don't catch a fever' — not only reflects the fragile state of his own health, but finds an exaggerated echo in Gresham's attitude to Helen's getting interested in the East End. Speaking to Mr Heatherley: 'Let her by all means disgust herself with a peep into these eastern dens of yours. I only hope she won't bring us some infectious disease here, that's all'.[25]

From Adam & Eve Court, Arthur moved first to Little St Andrew Street (Seven Dials) and then to Charlotte Place. The means of enacting the first of these moves seems to me the least geographically believable part of the novel. Arthur had been assaulted by his 'employer', Bill Blatherwick, whose character is much like Bill Sikes's in *Oliver Twist*, but took advantage of Bill's drunken stupor to escape, from somewhere in the vicinity of Saffron Hill, another allusion to *Oliver Twist*, whence he was rescued by Ned Quirk, daytime costermonger and resident of Little St Andrew Street, Seven Dials, who happened to be passing, presumably on his way back from his evening job selling baked potatoes at the corner of Old Street and City Road (the nearest major road intersection to Whitecross Street).[26] It is understandable that Ned's route home would take him near Saffron Hill; less believable that he would have chosen to ply his part-time trade so far from home, when there must have been numerous pitches in the West End or Covent Garden.

Given the eastward movement of 'East End' during the course of the nineteenth century, Whitecross Street in 1860 can be equated with Saffron Hill in the 1830s, the former just over half a mile east of the latter. Having stopped off in Saffron Hill for a farewell drink, Gissing could at last establish his own geography in the area in which he was more at home, a T-shaped locale extending north up Tottenham Court Road and west-east along the line of the 'New Road'

(Marylebone Road — Euston Road — Pentonville Road — City Road), the shabby margins of West End and City.

From Little St Andrew Street it is much more believable that Arthur should go on an errand that took him past Mr Tollady's shop in Charlotte Place. Socially and geographically, Charlotte Place was much like Colville Place, where Gissing lived for about nine months in 1878.[27] One is just west of Charlotte Street, the other immediately east. But unlike Colville Place, which is oriented east-west, the north-south orientation of Charlotte Place also offered a geographically logical route for Mr Gresham to follow, wanting to avoid the crowds on main roads through the West End, on his way home from the Strand to his house on Portland Place.[28] So Mr Gresham could see Arthur's artwork displayed in Tollady's window and the reconnection between Helen and Arthur was made possible.

Arthur's next moves, first to Gower Place, then to Huntley Street, and then to Islington, even more closely paralleled Gissing's own moves during 1878 and 1879.[29] Only Edward Street, off Hampstead Road, was omitted, and Hampstead Road played other roles than residence in *Workers*.[30] But we should pause for a moment in Gower Place and Huntley Street.

Gissing first situates Arthur and Carrie in separate rooms in the vulgar Mrs Pettindund's lodging house in Gower Place. Next, he moves them, first singly and then united in marital discord, to Huntley Street. Arthur marries Carrie in the hope of rescuing her from the bad company she has fallen into while lodging at Mrs Pettindund's. They move into Mrs Oaks' very respectable lodgings where Carrie not only starts to invite her friends round while Arthur is at work, but also shows signs of the addiction to alcohol which plagued Gissing's own first wife. It's not long before Mrs Oaks confronts Arthur: 'I shall be obliged to ask you to find other lodgings... the character of my house is being damaged. These girls that come so often to see your wife have such a very — unrespectable appearance ... I shall have my house empty if it goes on.'[31] This is set around 1870 and written in 1879. Twenty years later, Charles Booth's research assistant, George Duckworth, visited Bloomsbury in the company of a local police officer, in the process of updating the Booth poverty map. When they got to Huntley Street, Duckworth wrote: 'no prostitutes. In a working-class street like this the inhabitants won't let any prostitutes come, if they do, they complain to the agent at once and he turns them out.'[32]

Arthur's later moves replicated the footloose and coincidental nature of working-class mobility in Victorian London. When Carrie leaves him for the temptations of Soho, he moves to a garret in Islington. From there he is directed by a chance encounter while sitting at the reservoir in Pentonville Road (Claremont Square) to seek employment on Edgware Road, the farthest west that the novel ventured, and he found lodgings in Chapel Street.[33] Chapel Street resurfaced in Gissing's life a decade later as the site of cheap restaurants to which he would adjourn from his flat in Cornwall Residences; and as a result of these visits he was to discover Oxford & Cambridge Mansions, newly erected in the early 1880s just south of Chapel Street, and destined to play a critical role in *The Whirlpool*.[34]

Arthur's next move took him back from the far west to the East End, to lodgings with the Vennings, but only thanks to his coincidental rescue by his working-class radical friend, Will Noble, whose own lodgings on a side-street south of the Strand were conveniently on Arthur's route intending to commit suicide by drowning himself in the Thames. To be fair, Gissing depicts Arthur as deliberately visiting several sites in his personal history as he rambled from Chapel Street to the Thames, and almost willing Noble to emerge from his lodgings at just the right moment, an unlikely 'act of God' for the rationalist Gissing to contrive, although, as things turn out, it is only a temporary stay of execution, so perhaps not such a beneficent act after all.[35] But it is also fortuitous that in a city of four million people, Noble, living in the West End, should be so familiar with the Vennings, living in the East End.

Finally, during the course of 1872, Arthur, reunited with Carric, moved house so often that the narrator could not be bothered to enumerate all their lodgings: first to two rooms 'in a quiet little street in Hampstead,' then to Highgate, then 'repeatedly, coming at each time nearer to the town, for the sake of the increased privacy which — paradoxical as the assertion seems — a crowded neighbourhood secured for them.'[36] This is one of Gissing's most acute geographical observations, indicating the different forms of privacy in the nineteenth-century city.[37] We can contrast the privacy of suburban domesticity, exemplified by Helen's residence in 'Holly Cottage', Highbury, a privacy which depended on respectability, with the privacy afforded by neighbours who turned a blind eye or were simply oblivious to nonconforming behaviour, which was the privacy that Gissing craved in his own life with Nell, and that Arthur desired in his life with Carrie. The suburbs were often represented as 'anonymous' (implying that they displayed few unique characteristics which differentiated one suburb or one suburban street from another), but in the density and transiency of the inner city, it was the population who could be anonymous, who could 'disappear' from the consciousness of their neighbours, much as Nathaniel Hawthorne had first sketched in his short story, 'Wakefield' (1835).[38]

Arthur had also tried Hampstead and Highgate because they were close to 'nature' and he hoped the natural world would have a reforming influence on Carrie. But Carrie's reaction was to rate 'the grandeur of a sunset' as only 'almost as pretty as the theaytre'; 'when amid delightful country scenes she yearned for the lights of the shops and the coarse tumult of the pavement'.[39] Another advantage of Hampstead and Highgate was their remoteness from Carrie's old haunts and old friends: geography mattered in terms of time and distance from Soho, where she had been living while she and Arthur had been apart. Their return to the more 'private' environment of Camden Town also restored Carrie's access to temptation. It is geographically reasonable that, straying back into Tottenham Court Road from Camden Town, Carrie is reunited with her friend from Soho days, Polly Hemp.[40]

From lodgings in Camden Town, Arthur determined to make a new start, by way of an anonymous — and presumably very private — hotel in Charing Cross. Unlike 'Wakefield,' Arthur means his disappearance to be permanent. Thence by trains to Manchester and Liverpool, and a crossing on the Cunarder 'Parthia' from Liverpool to America, Arthur finally disappears in the waters of Niagara.

The 'Parthia' was a regular on transatlantic crossings between Liverpool and Boston and New York from its launch in 1870 until its transfer to other duties in 1883, with a capacity of 150 first-class and, more relevant to both Gissing and Arthur, 1031 third-class passengers.[41] The final chapter of *Workers* begins in Liverpool a few days before Christmas, 1872, as the 'Parthia' leaves for New York. The *Times* reported that the 'Parthia' called at Queenstown, Ireland, on 22nd December 1872 en route to New York, indicating that the vessel really did leave from Liverpool a few days before Christmas.[42] Pierre Coustillas speculated in his Introduction to the Harvester edition of *Workers* that the 'Parthia' may have been familiar to Gissing as the vessel which conveyed him from Liverpool to Boston in 1876.[43] The 'Parthia' sailed from Liverpool to Boston on 29th August, arriving in Boston on 10th September, and Bouwe Postmus notes in his Introduction to Gissing's 'American Notebook' that 'Mr Gissing' was named on the passenger list published in the *Boston Evening Transcript* on 11th September.[44]

Journeys: 2: Some London walks

I have devoted most of this article to the geography of Arthur's life in London but, as I indicated earlier, there are also individual journeys on which Gissing sends his characters, and thinking about them, too, offers valuable insights into how Gissing utilised space and place, and how he conceived of London's social geography. Consider, for example, Arthur and Tollady's Sunday afternoon walk from Charlotte Place eastward to Whitecross Street. The western part of this route is left unspecified, merely 'Citywards'.[45] This returns us again to *Oliver Twist*, for it is an intriguing mirror-image of Oliver's early morning 'expedition' with Bill Sikes, which Dickens charts in great detail, through Bethnal Green, Finsbury and Smithfield, all the way to Holborn. Then, in Moretti's words, 'the novel skips several miles' before continuing through the outer suburbs of west London.[46] Gissing's version in the reverse direction — an education in poverty rather than a plundering of wealth — skips the mile from its starting point in Charlotte Place to Smithfield, before picking up the route 'crossing Smithfield Market' and then following its protagonists' progress eastward 'in great detail'.

In the mid-1860s, when this scene is set, the old live-meat market, which Oliver had experienced — an amalgam of filth, mire, reeking bodies, whistling, barking, bellowing, bleating, grunting, squealing, swearing, quarrelling, whooping and yelling — had been closed for

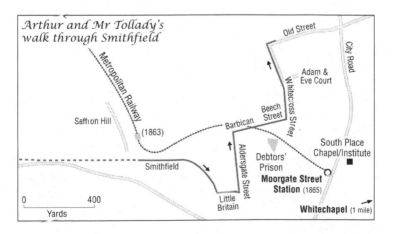

Arthur and Mr Tollady's walk through Smithfield

65

a decade. The date of Arthur and Tollady's walk is not specified, but it seems likely to have been before November 1868 when Horace Jones's new Central Market buildings had been completed.[47] Smithfield would have been waste ground (or, at most, a building site), probably empty and devoid of life on a Sunday afternoon, an ideal *tabula rasa* for Tollady's homily on the '*advance*' of humanity, and on how the martyrs of Smithfield — Protestants burnt at the stake under 'Bloody Mary' in the 1550s — were to be pitied rather than admired for adhering to their — to Tollady — irrational beliefs.[48] Moving on through Little Britain, a necessary deviation from a due eastward route, reflecting the labyrinth of alleys between Smithfield and Aldersgate Street, into Barbican, then Beech Street, they arrive at Whitecross Street. For Gissing and Arthur, this offers the opportunity to reprise the story so far, as necessary punctuation in the sprawling expanse of *Workers* as it was for Wagner, periodically, in the course of the 'Ring' (first performed in its entirety at Bayreuth in August 1876, less than a year before Wagner's visit to England in May 1877, an event anticipated in William's letter to George the previous month).[49] But for Tollady, Whitecross Street signifies the Debtors' Prison, opened in 1815 but near to closure by the time of Arthur and Tollady's walk. For Tollady, debt is to prove fatal. He dies of a heart attack when his home and shop is threatened with repossession.[50]

In revisions of *Workers* that Gissing began to sketch in the 1890s, the whole of the content of this walk is deleted. Instead, after starting out 'Citywards', we learn that 'they kept on till they reached the high street of Whitechapel', and it is there rather than in 'the more open neighbourhood of Old Street' that Tollady offers his next exhortation to Arthur to 'Paint a faithful picture of this crowd we have watched, be a successor of Hogarth...'[51] This is an excision and a relocation identical to those in *The Unclassed*, updating the geography of poverty from its 1860s–70s to its 1890s setting.[52]

On another of Arthur's walks — his first suicide mission from Chapel Street to the Thames south of the Strand — he passes the Marylebone Road workhouse at 'the time when the "casuals" were beginning to assemble in order to seek admittance for the night', a scene that had been vividly depicted by Luke Fildes, first in his engraving, 'Houseless and Hungry', published in the first issue of *The Graphic* in December 1869, and then in an oil painting, 'Applicants for Admission to a Casual Ward', exhibited at the Royal Academy in 1874.[53] The article accompanying the engraving stressed that these were real people drawn from life, each with their own tragic history. For Gissing, and Arthur, fear of having to resort to the workhouse was a very personal anxiety: 'Never, never!'[54]

Next, Arthur turns down Tottenham Court Road, left to revisit Huntley Street (his home with Carrie), right to Charlotte Place (Tollady and Pether), and so to a street between the Strand and the river (Noble), paying his last respects to each in turn. This north-south route, impossible to plot in its details in the period before Charing Cross Road was cut through the area, simplifying the labyrinth of narrow streets and alleys, constitutes a critical hinge in the geography of London. It is also the route followed, in reverse, by Gresham going from the Strand to Portland Place via Rathbone Place, and by Arthur going from Little St Andrew Street to Rathbone Place, and — if he ever bothered to attend lectures — by Augustus Whiffle going between his lodgings on University Street and King's College. It returns us to Moretti's idea of a 'third London.'

Gissing's 'Third London'

Moretti comments on *Oliver Twist*: 'Two half-Londons, that do not add up to a whole.' The two halves 'may touch briefly and in secret, like Rose and Nancy, at midnight, on the no-man's land of London Bridge: but it's only a moment (that will cost Nancy's life). If a novel focuses on one half of London, it simply cannot *see* the other half, nor represent the crossing of the border between them.'[55] But in later novels, Dickens unifies the two halves, finding — again to quote Moretti — that 'the result is *more* than the sum of its parts. London becomes not only a larger city (obviously enough), but a more *complex* one; allowing for richer, more unpredictable interactions.'[56] Moretti's 'third London' is a geographical wedge that holds the extremes of East End and West End together, and a social wedge of the growing middle class, *'a class in the middle'*.[57]

In *Workers in the Dawn*, Gissing's 'third London' extends through Bloomsbury and Fitzrovia to Covent Garden and the Strand. It is also a liminal zone, far more impermeable to the rich than to the poor. There is a self-imposed ban on the part of the middle classes about crossing the divide — on grounds of 'repulsion'. We cannot imagine that Mr Gresham, fearful of 'the Orient', has ever *visited* the East End, while Mrs Cumberbatch seems to have a kind of transit visa allowing her to reach the far end of Mile End Road *by omnibus* without ever having to alight en route — much like Engels's Manchester merchants who commuted between suburban home and city-centre office without ever seeing or coming into contact with the slums hidden behind the main streets along which they travelled by bus or carriage.[58] Charles Booth's Poverty Map shows Whitechapel Road and Commercial Road coloured in the pinks and reds of tradesmen's prosperity; the blues and blacks of poverty are hidden away on the back streets. But it's equally the case that the puritan middle-class outliers in the East End are repelled by the loose-living reputation of West Enders. Mr Heatherley is as ignorant of Portland Place as Mr Gresham is of Whitecross Street.[59] Among the working classes, however, the boundary is much more permeable. Will Noble (living south of the Strand) and the Vennings (East End) are in close contact; and Carrie,

Mrs Pole and Polly Hemp have no inhibitions about travelling anywhere east or north of Soho. The rich are more mobile nationally and on the continent: Helen, Maud and their fathers variously make trips to Dorset, Scarborough in Yorkshire, Tübingen in Germany, Paris, Mentone in the south of France and, prospectively, Russia. Yet the poor are more mobile *within* London, but also, at least the men, globally: as a young man, Tollady went travelling for 'three whole years' through Europe, Africa, Asia and North America.[60] Arthur replicates the American part of his journey at the close of the novel. Each is searching for the 'happy land, far, far away', *home*comings which they never achieve.[61]

For Gissing, geography was a matter of factual knowledge;[62] but — probably not consciously — he practised geography on almost every page of his writing. *Workers in the Dawn* may not be imbued with the logic of the railway timetable as were later books like *The Odd Women* and *The Whirlpool*,[63] but it is still a novel in which geography shapes the plot, and in which interpretation can be informed by our knowledge of geography.

[1] The Oxford World's Classics edition of *Mrs Dalloway* (2000), based on the Hogarth Press edition of 1942, includes a map on pages lx-lxi; in the Penguin edition (1992), the map is on pages vi-vii.
[2] The Blackwell edition of *Mrs Dalloway* (for Shakespeare Head Press, 1996) includes an annotated map on p. xxxiv. Note that there are some quite crude published maps of the characters' journeys, in D. Dowling, *Mrs Dalloway: Mapping Streams of Consciousness* (Boston, MA: Twayne, 1991), pp. 53-5, and online in E.K. Sparks, 'The London Walks of *Mrs Dalloway*', http://hubcap.clemson.edu/~sparks/TVSeminar/dallwalkmap.html (consulted 22 June 2010).
[3] Franco Moretti, *Atlas of the European Novel*, 1800–1900 (London: Verso, 1998), Chapter 2.
[4] *Ibid.*, p. 115.

[5] George Gissing, *Isabel Clarendon* (1886), Vol. II, pp. 91, 118, 120, 163. Gissing himself never lived as far north as the north end of Camden Town, but he would have known the area from his time spent in lodgings in Edward Street (June-Nov. 1879) and Rutland Street (Sept.-Dec. 1884), both just west of Hampstead Road; while the Chelsea location is precisely where Gissing lived – Oakley Crescent – from September 1882 to May 1884. Note, too, Gabriel's two paintings: 'a portion of an East End market-street at night'; and 'a little girl standing before a shop-window, and looking at an open illustrated paper which was exposed there' (p. 171). The first of these seems informed by Gissing's visit to the East End in February 1883, but is also matched by illustrations of East End scenes reproduced in, for example, the *Graphic*. The latter recalls paintings by genre artists such as Macduff, Houghton, or even Frith.

[6] Richard Dennis, 'George Gissing and the "Other" East End' in Christine Huguet, ed., *Writing Otherness: The Pathways of George Gissing's Imagination* (Haren, NL: Equilibris, 2011), pp. 35-48.

[7] George Gissing, *Workers in the Dawn* (ed. Debbie Harrison) (Brighton: Victorian Secrets, 2010). Subsequent references are to this edition.

[8] *Ibid.*, Chapter 5, p. 57.

[9] Paul F. Mattheisen, Arthur C. Young and Pierre Coustillas, eds, *The Collected Letters of George Gissing Volume II* (Athens, OH: Ohio UP, 1991), p. 121 (Letter to Ellen, 27 February 1883).

[10] *Workers*, Chapter 25, p. 301. The line was opened to Liverpool Street in 1875 and to Aldgate in 1876: see Christian Wolmar, *The Subterranean Railway* (London, 2004). It is possible, therefore, that Gissing, who did not conduct research for Workers in the way that he did for later slum novels such as *Thyrza* and *The Nether World*, might have assumed that Helen could travel all the way to Aldgate, which was within easy walking distance of Whitechapel; but the implication of his 1883 letter is that he was not familiar with Whitechapel in 1879 when he was writing *Workers*.

[11] *Workers*, Chapter 18, p. 199.

[12] History of the South Place Ethical Society, http://www. ethicalsoc.org.uk/spes/about (consulted 22 June 2010).

[13] Paul F. Mattheisen, Arthur C. Young and Pierre Coustillas, eds, *The Collected Letters of George Gissing Volume I* (Athens, OH: Ohio UP, 1990), pp. 153-5 (Letter to Algernon,

19 February 1879).

[14] *Workers*, Chapter 25, p. 295.

[15] For online versions of Charles Booth's Poverty Map, see
http://www.umich.edu/~risotto/ (1889 map) and http://booth.
lse.ac.uk/ (1899 revision). Unfortunately, both maps
postdate programmes of slum clearance and of railway
construction (such as the building of Liverpool Street
Station in the early 1870s), which also targeted slums; and
Booth omitted to survey areas inside the City of London.
Nevertheless, the maps give a good sense of the continuing
proximity of rich and poor in late nineteenth-century inner
London.

[16] *Workers*, Chapters 29-30, pp. 355-6. On Gissing's later
experience of the Oxford Music Hall, see Pierre Coustillas
(ed.), *London and the Life of Literature in Late Victorian
England: The Diary of George Gissing, Novelist* (Hassocks:
Harvester, 1978), p. 226 (24 Sept 1890); for alternative
interpretations of this event, see Paul F. Mattheisen,
Arthur C. Young and Pierre Coustillas, eds, *The Collected
Letters of George Gissing Volume IV* (Athens, OH: Ohio UP,
1993) p. 241; Paul Delany, *George Gissing: A Life* (London:
Weidenfeld & Nicolson, 2008), p. 177.

[17] *Workers*, Chapter 17, p. 190.

[18] *Ibid.*, Chapter 26, p. 304-5.

[19] *Ibid.*, Chapters 19-20 and 31, pp. 217, 222, 369, 376.

[20] David L. Pike, 'Modernist space and the transformation of
Underground London' in Pamela K. Gilbert, ed., *Imagined
Londons* (Albany NY: State University of New York Press,
2002), pp. 101-19; Ken Garland, *Mr Beck's Underground
Map* (Harrow: Capital Transport Publishing, 1994).

[21] On the Cross Act, see Anthony S. Wohl, *The Eternal Slum:
Housing and Social Policy in Victorian London* (London:
Edward Arnold, 1977); J.A. Yelling, *Slums and Slum
Clearance in Victorian London* (London: Allen & Unwin,
1986).

[22] London County Council, *The Housing Question in London*
(London: P. S. King and Son, 1900), pp. 135-40; Peabody
Donation Fund, Governors Minutes and Annual Reports,
London Metropolitan Archives, ACC/3445/PT/01/007/01.

[23] 'Artisans' Dwellings Act,' *Times*, 17 April 1877, p. 4, 23
April 1877, p. 4, 26 April 1877, p. 6; 'The Evictions in St
Luke's,' *Lloyd's Weekly Newspaper*, 15 April 1877;
'Improvement of St Luke's,' *Standard*, 16 April 1877, p. 3;
'London's Courts and Alleys,' *Standard*, 20 August 1875, p.
2, 25 August 1875, p. 2 (Old Nichol Street), 28 August 1875,

p. 3 (Seven Dials), 2 Sept 1875, p. 3 (Golden Lane).

[24] Bouwe Postmus (ed.), *An Exile's Cunning: Some Private Papers of George Gissing* (Wormerveer, NL: Stichting Uitgeverij Noord-Holland, 1999), p. 58; Mattheisen et al., *Collected Letters Volume I*, p. 94 (Letter from William, 16 June 1878). See also p. 293 (Letter to Frederic Harrison, 23 July 1880), for Gissing's assurance of the authenticity of his accounts of low life, having walked 'along Whitecross Street or around Seven Dials late on Saturday night.'

[25] *Workers*, Chapter 17, p. 198.

[26] *Ibid.*, Chapters 5 and 6, pp. 58-9, 64-5.

[27] For Gissing's own accounts of Colville Place, see 'The Last Half-Crown' in Pierre Coustillas (ed.), *George Gissing: Essays & Fiction* (Baltimore: Johns Hopkins Press, 1970), pp. 179-85; George Gissing, *The Private Papers of Henry Ryecroft* (London: Constable, 1903), Spring, X.

[28] *Workers*, Chapter 15, p. 167.

[29] Robin Woolven, 'George Gissing's London Residences 1877-1891,' *Gissing Journal*, October 2004, pp. 5-15.

[30] For example, as the route of Tollady's funeral, *Workers*, Chapter 23, p. 270.

[31] *Workers*, Chapter 34, p. 416.

[32] Charles Booth Online Archive (http://booth.lse.ac.uk/) Police Notebooks, B355, p. 119; see also Richard Dennis, 'The place of Bloomsbury in the novels of George Gissing,' *Opticon1826*, 7 (Autumn 2009), online at http://www.ucl.ac.uk/opticon1826/archive/issue7/Articles/Article_Dennis_Gissing.pdf.

[33] *Workers*, Chapter 35, p. 433-4.

[34] Coustillas, *London and the Life of Literature in Late Victorian England: The Diary of George Gissing, Novelist*, pp. 29 (27 May 1888), 144 (18 March 1889), 151 (18 May 1889), 160 (20 August 1889); Mattheisen et al., *Collected Letters Volume IV*, p. 129 (Letter to Margaret, 20 October 1889).

[35] *Workers*, Chapter 35, pp. 437-41.

[36] *Ibid.*, Chapter 45, pp. 561, 569-70.

[37] Donald J. Olsen, *The Growth of Victorian London* (London: Batsford, 1976).

[38] Nathaniel Hawthorne, 'Wakefield', *The New England Magazine* (May 1835), reprinted in *Twice-Told Tales* Volume I (Boston: Houghton Mifflin, 1900), pp. 172-86.

[39] *Workers*, Chapter 45, p. 564.

[40] *Ibid.*, Chapter 45, pp. 570-1.

[41] 'Ships named Parthia', http://www.parthia.com/ships/

parthia_01.htm (consulted 27 June 2010).

[42] *Times*, 23 December 1872, p. 3.

[43] Pierre Coustillas, 'Introduction', in *George Gissing, Workers in the Dawn* (Brighton: Harvester, 1985), p. xxii.

[44] *Liverpool Mercury*, 22 August 1876; Postmus, *An Exile's Cunning*, p. 5. For recent research on the 'Parthia' which goes far beyond my own scanning of online newspapers, see Marcus Neacey, 'George Gissing's Voyage to America and the Hazardous Career of the "Good ship Parthia,"' *Gissing Journal*, July 2010, pp. 23-33.

[45] *Workers*, Chapter 11, p. 119.

[46] Moretti, *Atlas of the European Novel*, p. 86. Dickens has Oliver and Sikes starting from the vicinity of Bishopsgate: 'Turning down Sun Street and Crown Street, and crossing Finsbury Square, Mr Sikes struck, by way of Chiswell street, into Barbican: thence into Long Lane, and so into Smithfield...' (*Oliver Twist*, Chapter XXI, 'The Expedition').

[47] Walter Thornbury, *Old and New London Volume 2* (London: Cassell, 1878), pp. 491-6; online at http://www.british-history.ac.uk/report.aspx?compid=45117

[48] *Workers*, Chapter 11, p. 121.

[49] Mattheisen et al., *Collected Letters Volume I*, pp. 58-60 (Letter from William, 16 April 1877); Anne D. Sessa, *Richard Wagner and the English* (Cranbury NJ: Associated University Presses, 1979), Chapter 1. For Gissing's own, later, interest in Wagner, see Paul F. Mattheisen, Arthur C. Young and Pierre Coustillas, eds, *The Collected Letters of George Gissing Volume III* (Athens, OH: Ohio UP, 1992), pp. 117-23.

[50] *Workers*, Chapters 11 and 22, pp. 122, 256-61; Jerry White, *London in the Nineteenth Century* (London: Jonathan Cape, 2007), pp. 219-20.

[51] *Ibid.*, Chapter 11, pp. 122-3. On Gissing's deletions, see Coustillas's notes to the Harvester edition, pp. 159, 163.

[52] Dickens had re-located Fagin from Saffron Hill to Whitechapel in the course of *Oliver Twist* (and Oliver's 'expedition' had begun from Sikes's home in Bethnal Green). So it might be thought that in alluding to Whitechapel, Gissing was renewing his debt to Dickens. But if this was the case we would have expected the references to Whitechapel to have been included in the original versions of *Workers* and *The Unclassed*. Note, too, that Dickens does not use the term 'East End' to embrace Whitechapel or Bethnal Green. His only use of 'East-end' in a novel, in *Nicholas Nickleby* (1838-39), is to describe a

'deserted mansion' in Thames Street, i.e. in the vicinity of London Bridge, effectively confirming the westerly location of 'East End' at this time. On Gissing's revisions to *The Unclassed*, see Dennis, 'George Gissing and the "Other" East End.'

[53] *Workers*, Chapter 35, p. 437; Julian Treuherz, *Hard Times: Social Realism in Victorian Art* (London: Lund Humphries, 1987), Chapters 7 and 10.

[54] *Workers*, Chapter 35, p. 437.

[55] Moretti, *Atlas of the European Novel*, pp. 84-6.

[56] *Ibid.*, p. 86.

[57] *Ibid.*, p. 117.

[58] Friedrich Engels, *The Condition of the Working Class in England* (London: Grafton, 1969), pp. 79-80.

[59] *Workers*, Chapter 17, p. 195.

[60] *Ibid.*, Chapter 22, pp. 252-3.

[61] *Ibid.*, Chapters 5, 11 and 27, pp. 54, 122 and 325: the words of a Sunday School hymn sung by children playing in Whitecross Street, from which Gissing derived his original title for the novel: *Far, Far Away*. For Gissing's own thoughts on this title, see Mattheisen et al., *Collected Letters Volume I*, p. 215 (Letter to Algernon, 3 Nov 1879) and p. 229 (Letter to Algernon, 2 Jan 1880).

[62] See, for example Mattheisen et al., *Collected Letters Volume I*, p. 32 (Letter to Arthur Bowes, 24 May 1874), p. 135 (Letter to Algernon, 17 Dec 1878). Until circumstances forced him to sell them, Gissing had his own collection of Ordnance Survey maps: Mattheisen et al., *Collected Letters Volume IV*, p. 311 (Letter to Algernon, 25 July 1891).

[63] Lynne Hapgood, 'The literature of the suburbs: versions of repression in the novels of George Gissing, Arthur Conan Doyle and William Pett Ridge, 1890-1899', *Journal of Victorian Culture*, 5 (2000), pp. 303-5.

This article first appeared in *The Gissing Journal* (published by The Gissing Trust), Volume XLVI, Number 4, October 2010, and is reproduced with the editor's permission.

Ian Nairn:
taking Jack Kerouac
on the Road
Gillian Darley

In the early months of the Second World War, the ten-year old Ian Nairn bought himself a Michelin map. Sulkily confined to suburban Camberley, he immersed himself in a cartographic portrait of the Cherbourg and Rouen region (sheet 54). Finally, in the summer of 1948, he was there, on French soil. He remembered happily sitting beside his bike on a roadside verge, 'hazy with cider' but sobered by the thought that had he been just five years older, he would have seen Normandy under very different conditions.

At his best Ian Nairn was, by any reckoning, one of the great writers of the mid twentieth century. His field was, ostensibly, architecture and the built environment, but his range and reach were profound. In the preface to that still-sparkling and never bettered portrait of an immense city, *Nairn's London* (1966) he wrote that he sought 'character, or personality, or essence' which gave an 'internal reality of which beauty is only one facet.'

He travelled in search of a sense of place, those occurrences and meetings between terrain and territory that are more usually the result of happenstance rather than deliberation. But often, on arrival, he had to confront the absence of anything worthy of celebration — quite the reverse. He journeyed in introspective, often melancholy, mood with eyes and mind always alert, ever ready to celebrate the exceptional or the absurd, the vital or the simply commendable, or, if appropriate, to execrate without fear or favour.

A Meteor pilot stationed at RAF Horsham St Faith in the early 1950s, Flight Officer Nairn had already put his navigational skills (and his jet fighter) to unorthodox use. As he flew over Norfolk and Suffolk, he passed the time building up an inventory of obscure country houses, in particular those designed by John Soane. On his third sortie over Earsham Hall, then a boys' school, he had spotted Soane's lost Music Room, hidden in the bushes. Like a latter-day Alain-Fournier in pursuit of something lovely briefly glimpsed, he then returned on foot, and pushed through the shrubbery to find the exquisite garden pavilion, virtually intact.

From an address in the lugubrious sounding Unthank Road, Norwich he shared his latest coup (and fuzzy photographs) with the redoubtable Dorothy Stroud, the Inspectress of Sir John Soane's Museum and John Summerson's deputy curator. Evidently impressed by Nairn's unusually effective approach, she told him how 'when snooping over a hedge' she too had often 'wished for a pair of wings!' One weekend, after duly warning her of the twin rigours of Norfolk in March and the foibles of their ancient car, Nairn and his wife Joan drove Miss Stroud around the Norfolk countryside in a 1926 Austin.

In 1955 the Architectural Press published *Outrage,* Nairn's furious polemic against the second-rate in the everyday environment, which had begun life as a series of articles in the *Architectural Review.* He had resigned his RAF commission in 1953 after two 'eventful' years and escaped to London, where still clad in his RAF greatcoat, he continually door-stepped the editors of the *AR.* Before long the co-proprietor, joint editor and idiosyncratic choreographer of the magazine's campaigns, Hubert de Cronin Hastings, capitulated to his overtures and Nairn was taken onto the staff, nominally employed as production editor — his role soon being shuffled onto other shoulders and allowing him full rein as a journalist. The elegant early 18th century terrace that housed the Architectural Press at Queen Anne's Gate included a Victorian pub that had been, eccentrically, reconstructed in the basement. The Bride of Denmark was a particularly congenial addition to the working environment for the beer-loving Nairn.

The field of battle for *Outrage* was based upon a line drawn down the length of a map of England and Scotland, 'a line as straight as main roads permit from the bottom to the top.' The route chosen 'may claim the doubtful distinction of being the first example of a travel agent's trip in reverse — picking out the bad, not the good.' Nairn drove the 400 miles from Southampton to Carlisle (or more precisely Gretna), presumably in a more serviceable vehicle than the Austin, and photographed whatever caught his eye, most of it hideous or, at least, inappropriate. The section titled 'Route Book' sandwiched a running commentary and captions (on coloured paper) between a dense array of small photographs, interspersed by his colleague Gordon Cullen's drawings and a continuous map, like a running header along the top of successive pages. The graphics were brilliant, the message grim. This was 'subtopia' or, put with his typical baldness, 'the abyss'.

The angry, abrasive language anchored by the snapshot images, (aerial shots were often by *AR* photographer Bill Toomey, piloted by Nairn) and given extra impact by the bravura design of the pages gave Nairn and Cullen, an architect and associate editor at the *AR*, the status of revolutionary, even prophetic figures in the USA. There, attention was turning to the ramifications of a huge road building and slum clearance project as well as the rectification of earlier low quality building programmes. Next, Nairn and Cullen produced *Counter-Attack,* a rather more practical publication. Operating from the portentous sounding 'Counter-Attack Bureau' (in reality little more than an in-tray on a desk at Queen Anne's Gate), they were becoming internationally sought-after authorities.

The opinionated and graphically sophisticated issues of *AR* were held in great esteem in the USA. Soon reciprocal mentions in friendly publications turned to invitations

77

and in early 1957 Nairn made his first ten-day long trip, city to city — visiting New York, Louisville, Chicago, San Francisco and San Antonio — in order to produce an AR style insert of captioned townscape views for a special issue of *Fortune* magazine. The following year, 1958, the essays were combined in a book titled *The Exploding City*. The images were Gordon Cullen's drawings after Nairn's photographs since Cullen did not travel by air. Nairn's contribution was set within Jane Jacobs' 'Downtown is for People' — she, since 1956, having been the editor responsible for urban renewal coverage in *Fortune*'s sister magazine at Time-Life, *Architectural Forum*. The book made considerable waves; what was a business magazine up to questioning the unlimited physical expansion of a country boasting a confident economy or, for that matter undercutting those professionals, the architects and engineers, who were purposefully remodelling the urban landscape?

Jacobs' keen critical mind and resistance to professional special pleading came into their own with her piece, the argument immediately evident in the title. Nairn, who stayed with her in New York, had found someone after his own cast of mind and almost as blunt. Although they soon took different professional paths, for a brief time they were complementary voices. Jane Jacobs commented that Nairn's viewpoint 'arrived at from the aesthetic side' coincided largely with hers 'arrived at from the sociological side'. Nairn found his subject matter as he journeyed, and saw interconnections wherever he looked. As he was to write, splendidly, of London 'all the attributes of the capital have piled on to this shallow basin of gravel like rugby players in a scrum, kicking and elbowing each other out of the way'. Jacobs found her arguments, no less pungently put, by immersing herself in a place or site, and then finding its particular qualities for those who lived and worked there.

Nairn, a voracious reader, was becoming increasingly curious about the USA and what it might offer. So it was that, thanks to Jacobs, Chadbourne Gilpatric, an associate director of the Humanities Division of the Rockefeller Foundation found himself in the Bride of Denmark ('as delightful as it is surprising') in March 1959 talking to Nairn, their conversation lubricated by 'occasional beers on the house'. Gilpatric was looking for 'other Lewis Mumfords, who could bring critical philosophical and historical background to bear on problems of urban planning.' Jane Jacobs' experience in the urban renewal field, her contacts with academics, professionals and journalists, had made her a trusted, if informal, referee to Gilpatric since the Rockefeller Foundation was funding her own work, to become *The Death and Life of Great American cities* (1961). Ironically, in the circumstances, Mumford who knew nothing of her years as an editor at *Architectural Forum*, reviewed her book with withering scorn, referring to 'Mother Jacobs' home remedies.' In the end it harmed his reputation more than hers.

The eventual outcome of the London meeting, after much correspondence and various proposals, was Nairn's arrival in New York in November 1959 to take up his own Rockefeller Foundation grant towards a publication with the working title of 'Townscape USA'. Again, Nairn stayed with Jacobs. At this early point, Gilpatric understood Nairn to be planning some short trips to 'selected American cities', before returning to the USA again, in May, with Cullen. In these days Nairn converted or subverted this scheme into a massive road trip, the 'grand slam' as he called it, three months on the road.

Gilpatric, for all his background in wartime intelligence, in the OSS, followed by three years in the CIA, seemed to have been gently hoodwinked by Nairn, a twenty-eight year old novice. Despite the emphasis laid by the grant giving bodies in these nervous Cold War years that their overseas recipients should return with the most positive and wide ranging accounts of the USA, its breadth, charm and prosperity, not merely its struggling, ghettoized cities, Nairn far outran any itinerary that might have been suggested to him. His 1952 Plymouth soft top, bought for $295 and brought up to scratch for another $200, took him 10,000 miles around the USA, entirely without trouble. The 800 miles to Carlisle and back had been a weekend jaunt by comparison.

He travelled around the East Coast, then from Philadelphia to Los Angeles, via Chicago, coming back via Texas and the Deep South. As he went Nairn dug into modern fiction (and, no doubt, film) to gain a sense of place. American novels were, he considered, as good as any being written and 'work on purely American terms.' John O'Hara's *Ten North Frederick* and James Jones' *Some Came Running* conjured up localities but he considered the towns as undifferentiated as Greyhound waiting rooms. He had higher hopes of beat writing. Jack Kerouac's recently published *On the Road* 'asks to be read as a novel' writes James Campbell 'not as a minutely adjusted slice of life' but that was not how Nairn approached it. Nor was a book about the vicissitudes of intense friendship to be read alone. The itinerant outsider view, necessarily Nairn's in these long, solitary weeks, made him increasingly desperate.

On the Road (written in 1951, but not published until 1957) is an odyssey, in which the rackety characters bounce from corner to corner of the USA, landing on unsuspecting relatives and friends in New Orleans, Denver, San Francisco, Manhattan and elsewhere. Between the lines, the cities and neighbourhoods emerge but seen through a haze, vestigial and revealing all too

little beyond the growing claustrophobia and destructiveness of the relationships between characters.

Kerouac had intended to follow Route 6, ('one long red line... from the tip of Cape Cod clear to Ely, Nevada and there dipped down to Los

Angeles') but the journeys he threaded through his novel actually criss-crossed America randomly, more like the progress of a travelling salesman as he put it. It was Mexico, its 'reality' that finally spoke to Kerouac. Nothing beat about that discovery, Nairn remarked, in the 'touching, whole-hearted acceptance of this pattern and vitality.' It was almost as if, when Kerouac found that authenticity, his acolyte Nairn (who never in fact got to Mexico) could stop worrying.

Nairn took Route 66 from Chicago west, as well as 6 and 1 and 22 and many more. He often looked at cities from Kerouac's perspective. Why should Denver be, for an American, 'a glory of excitement, a mixture of Amsterdam, Chartres and Naples', Nairn wondered. Why could Denver not stand for itself? A sense of place 'is something which man cannot afford to do without.' Fragmentation of the man-made environment would lead to an equivalent sense of disorientation in the population. 'No matter', Kerouac had written, 'the road is life'.

The American Landscape was published five years afterwards. In retrospect Ian Nairn's most memorable day in the USA was a long drive west through the panhandle of Oklahoma and northwest Texas, 'made memorable because of the fact that — almost alone in America — each tiny town had identity of the most breathtaking and sublime sort' provided by the succession of grain elevators, glinting on the horizon at every rise in the interminable ribbon of road. Only 'functional accidents' could tie such a scene together, in Nairn's view. The banks of silos (admired by every European modernist, starting with le Corbusier), the water towers and courthouse squares were proudly dominant, emphatic amidst the negligible.

He went to Phoenix, San Diego and Pensacola, to St Louis and Louisville. In Tallahassee he admired (and photographed) the full extent of the expressway rolling, purposefully, towards the state capitol. He bemoaned Frank Lloyd Wright's Price Tower in Bartlesville,

Oklahoma, set pointlessly like a 'needle among the subdivisions.' Hardly any of his responses were predictable, except perhaps his absorption of the 'over-ripe' architecture of Charleston and Savannah. San Antonio bewitched him, its river looping gently through the city and providing a thin ribbon of town garden, giving it a 'connected, organic pattern' (though he must have also shared something of Kerouac's delight in its illicit near-Mexican air, 'dark, and mysterious, and buzzing'). He celebrated Chicago, with a Piranesian subterranean riverside and its inside-outside world ('printing presses, bowels of buildings') set against a rugged skyline revealed by the Loop and yet, he wondered despairingly, 'for every few yards like this, in America, how many tens of thousands of miles are there of screaming monotony?' All the more meaningless, judged by that reality, was the contrived New England village ('the Nemesis of Old Sturbridge') or the ersatz adobe nonsense of Santa Fe.

Jane Jacobs had shared insights with her English visitor. In *Death and Life* she celebrated the qualities of Boston North End, no slum but 'one of the most human places in America', and the seemingly threatened potential of Pittsburgh, which had given her 'my first inkling about the powerful effects of certain kinds of functional mixtures in the city.' The goal of his own book, Nairn wrote 'could be described as giving each place, in its own terms and ways, the equivalent of the human excitement of the North End and the topographical excitement of Pittsburgh.' He gave Jane Jacobs no credit.

From time to time in the book and, increasingly in his later journalism, Nairn put himself centre stage. He'd been profoundly disturbed by the atmosphere of hatred in the Deep South, 'for Limey strangers as for blacks', (but exempted New Orleans). On his own trip, the nadir might have been Christmas Day in Pershing Square in downtown Los Angeles, feeling lonely and laden with emotional worries. It had been raining, then the Californian sun came out to find 'nobody here but us ...

derelicts and lushes united just for the day'. He had photographed the scene. In that 'unfairly derided city... the place that everyone says has no centre' he'd joined a group of people whole-heartedly 'enjoying their city.' Nairn, as his colleague Gordon Cullen recalled after his death, 'wore his emotions the way most people wear varicose veins.'

In many ways, what Nairn had proposed to the Rockefeller Foundation proved to be impossible. So different in every detail was the development and style of life of post-war North America that Nairn's criticism of the anomie of British suburbia, always in some way referring to an urban parent, could get no traction on American 'roadtown', where the nearest city boundary might be hundreds of miles distant and where neighbourhoods seemed to have popped up in the night. Even Nairn's hated local authorities had their intermittent justification. Writing later about Jean Renoir's *La Regle du Jour* he observed how even the stupidest set of rules can be 'given nobility' by the way they are carried out.

Nairn returned to the USA on several future occasions and was revising his attitudes all the time. In autumn 1960 he had written wrote a piece about Glasgow for *The Listener* (where much of his finest writing appeared). He likened it to 'the best parts of some American cities – Boston or Philadelphia' but compared to a walk in the street in Glasgow, so friendly in terms of 'person-to-person recognition' he recalled the 'many miles of American urban sidewalk' he had pounded, only to experience indifference or the 'mutual hate of cogs in a machine who know their plight but cannot escape it'.

By the late 1960s he was wondering, perhaps tempted in this direction by his old *AR* colleague and sparring partner Reyner Banham , if 'roadtown' might be considered 'a worthwhile animal in its own right — as long as it wasn't everywhere.' In the mid 1970s, he took a coast-to-coast trip on minor roads, from Washington DC to Seattle in a fortnight. 'I had a very personal reason for making this trip: to exorcise my dislike of America'. This time his journey was 'supremely happy'. He visited just two medium sized towns — Terre Haute, Indiana and Lincoln, Nebraska. West of Missouri the landscape provided 'one astonishment after another' and the towns were generous places to a passerby. Quintessentially to Nairn's taste were the chance contacts in small town bars, highly agreeable encounters, his 'ships in the night'.

In a piece for *Sunday Times,* where he ended his journalistic career before lapsing into a long wordless hiatus before dying from cirrhosis of the liver aged fifty-two, he remembered the great road trip as a grim journey, his paymasters at the Rockefeller Foundation angry that he had strayed so far off the prescribed route, and his unhappiness exacerbated by his emotional state (Nairn's first marriage was failing). *The American Landscape* can be seen as much a literary homage, an evocation of a continent, as the critical and practical report that the Foundation had hoped for. Nairn quoted William Blake, 'One law for the Lion & Ox is Oppression' and if, he wrote, his introduction 'begins to sound like a beat novel, it is no accident'.

So it is, surely, no accident that Kerouac's coda is so in tune with and so closely reflects Ian Nairn's formative American journey; 'when the sun goes down and I sit on the old broken-down river pier watching the long, long skies over New Jersey and sense all that raw land that rolls in one unbelievable huge bulge over to the West Coast, and all that road going, all the people dreaming in the immensity of it ... nobody, nobody knows what's going to happen to anybody beside the forlorn rage of growing old.'

My thanks to David McKie, with whom I plan to publish a celebratory anthology of Ian Nairn's best writing, to Graham Fisher in Chester, to Robert Elwall, Gaby Higgs, Susan Palmer, the Rockefeller Foundation and to Mathew Aitchison and fellow contributors to the Townscape symposium held in London in July 2011.

Wilford: an English village in the 1950s
Roberta Dewa

The Power House

This is how Wilford would have looked from space, in the 1950s: a tongue of land at the southern extremity of the city of Nottingham, formed by a meander in the River Trent; a pale blue meander thrown around the land like the loop of a skipping rope. A tongue of land pushing like a cheeky boy towards the city, but safe from it behind its water barrier. This tongue, or isthmus, is Wilford, a once-medieval village built in linear fashion along its main road, which branches out here and there into 1920s and 30s cul-de-sacs of neat brick semis, but keeps generally on a south to north course, hugging the west bank of the river as it heads for the tip of the tongue and the old Toll Bridge, the Victorian structure of brick and iron which bolts it to the world on the north side of the Trent.

To the east of the village, and bisecting the isthmus into west and eastern halves, is the almost dead-straight line of the railway embankment, carrying the goods and passengers of the Great Central Railway south to London, crossing the river by its own double bridge of massive metal piers and girder spans and dwarfing the Toll Bridge a hundred yards away. East again, and everything is green to the far shore of the isthmus: a green of fields and allotments and scrubland scrawled with the wavy lines of unofficial paths: paths to the willows along the river, paths to dens, paths to the arches of the railway viaduct, paths to the glassy water of the Ballast Hole, a lozenge of water left by a forgotten flood and stranded, like an Oxbow lake, in one of Wilford's fields. Around the fields are floodbanks of the earthen, informal variety, that are a part of our landscape, surrounding us like Dutch dykes, good vantage-points and boundary markers. On the river side of the floodbanks nearest the bridge are fields of ponies; to the east of the isthmus, beyond the railway line, the wilderness of paths and dens and undergrowth we call the Willowwoods, a name with surely deliberate echoes of Kenneth Grahame's Wild Wood. Here, where the land is vulnerable to inundation and thus unusable, we occasionally meet with Wilford's own incarnation of stoats and weasels.

Water. Without which Wilford would have been absorbed into the city long ago, without which it would have lost its village identity, its legends of fatalities on the ferry which served as conduit across the river until the bridge was built; its legends of drowned limp bodies lying in the riverside mortuary next to St Wilfrid's Church. Without which it would have held less holiday magnetism for the slum-dwellers of the Meadows, enjoying the otherness of the bridge crossing, the paying of the toll, the teas served from thatched cottages and cherry-eatings in the Vicarage garden. Water, without which the village residents would

not have had to move upstairs after many winters, but especially those of 1940 and 1947, while the Trent forsook its loop and moved in on the village, causing engineers to visit with levels and theodolites and to raise the floodbanks higher, felling the avenue of elms along the old Bee Bank and hoisting up its horizon with earth and stone and new techniques in concrete.

Water that divides us from the industry on the north side of the river, from the spinwheel of Clifton Colliery, the power station with its Art Deco brickwork, its tall chimneys with their pink evening glow, the long aeroplane hiss of sudden escapes of steam; that protects us from the dull controlled explosions and unexplained lightning flashes emanating from the Gun Factory. These places are of Wilford, but North Wilford, caught in the photographs of early village views as blurry backdrops, hard shapes softened out by lenses fixing on the small, the near, the picturesque, the rural. Existing in a kind of willed myopia, an uncorrected defect of vision that we all have.

Lenses that we need just to go about our daily business, in the 1950s, the 1960s. So many of us are short-sighted: my grandmother, my grandfather and my mother with their bottle glasses, the sepia-brown tint to protect their eyes from sun. Turn up any photograph of the Women's Institute or the Mothers' Union and there they are, beneath the candyfloss topping of best hats; the spectacles, some black severe National Health issue, most of them winged on the top edge of the frame, blue plastic flourishes turned upward at the end like surrogate eyebrows. Without them we do not see very far, maybe to the end of the avenue, maybe as far as Mr Pearce's flame of white hair as he reads the lesson; certainly not the numbers of the hymns or the sums on the blackboard, not as far as anything that changes, that cannot be remembered. Without them we can still walk through the village in soft focus, getting our bearings from the white front of Hunter's Farm as we pass it, the green pools of the village greens, the squat Georgian huddle of the Village Shop, where the week's grocery order is waiting for us in a basket.

And for everyday needs, Wilford provides: the sweetshop with its penny box full of liquorice and glass jars of Pineapple Chunks and Dolly Mixtures; the Village Hall where there are dances and Church socials; the pub

87

where the beer is brought by two splendid dray-horses that leave their steaming droppings in the road, shining brown like soft horse-chestnuts; the church, breasting the bend in the river like a lighthouse, for those occasions where change feels like continuity: birth, marriage, death.

Short sight keeps us content, thankful in a postwar world where there is so much to be thankful for. The two world war generations make do and mend, they cut their loaves of bread horizontally so that the slices are holed with the tracery of lace, they save brown paper and butter wrappers and light the stove with long coloured tapers. Their carbon footprints, supposing such a thing were known of in the fifties, would be light as air. Most of the villagers, including my own family, own no car; my family will never own one. And the Toll Bridge, its curlicues of ironwork corroding into rust-flowers beneath our feet, is already too weakened to support a bus; its weight limit falls year by year, four tons, two tons, Pedestrians Only. We are untroubled. We walk, as we have always done.

Violence on the
English Riviera
John Lucas

I

No, not Teddy Boys cutting up rough in a Torquay café.
Not Mods and Rockers going berserk on Goodrington
Sands. Not Skinheads terrorising Paignton Promenade.
The violence I have in mind took place some hundred and
fifty years ago and did far more damage to persons and
property than any gang warfare of more recent times can
lay claim to. Not that there's mention of such violence in
most histories of the bay, which emphasise a quality
Henry James might have called the 'record of the long,
safe centuries'. But, unlikely as it may seem, it happened.

Before I come to that, however, I need to provide the
setting. Torbay is a wide, concave curve of the Devon
coast, south facing, sheltered, its climate allowing the
growth of sub-tropical plant life. Poster campaigns of the
Great Western Railways and travel agencies used to
image this particular stretch of coastline as a stretch of
golden sand backed by red earth leading to lush upland,
spread before it a blue, unruffled sea fringed by palm
trees. 'The English Riviera', as it became known, was a
favoured watering-hole for the rich and the titled.
Violence here? Well, yes, although admittedly it
happened before Torquay became known as the Queen of
the English Riviera. Paignton, the town next along the
bay shore never had the same cachet. But in both towns
tranquillity was put at risk.

Tranquillity. This above all was the image of Torbay
sedulously fostered by those who, as the concept of
seaside holidays began to develop in the nineteenth
century, moved to take advantage of the bay's ideal
situation. But there was a problem. In fact, there were
two. The first was transport. Torbay was a long way from

89

London. London to Brighton was one thing. Even London to Weymouth was possible. Both seaside resorts became popular during regency times when Prinny's vast bulk — he weighed at least twenty stone — could be levered into a coach and for his better health removed from the capital. But London to Torquay?

It was the coming of the railway that solved that problem. But with it came another. Large numbers of summer visitors brought with them the need for improved street lighting. Mains gas was therefore required. And this inevitably created a third problem. To build the railway and dig the trenches for gas pipes you needed a sizeable work force. And it was the arrival of large numbers of navvies which led to three moments of real violence. They are all perfect examples of popular protest, or what the historian George Rudé called crowd riots, spontaneous outbursts against perceived injustice. They weren't the acts of a mob — led from above by an outsider with an ulterior motive for stirring up the local populace — even if that was how the press at the time described them.

I say 'if' because the evidence of press reports, assuming there to have been any, has disappeared along with the archives of *The Torquay Times*. Nor do any of the three major incidents feature in any account I've come across of nineteenth-century popular protest. The first time I heard of these riots was from my paternal grandfather, who came from Torquay itself. I know absolutely nothing about his forebears. I do, however, know that he married a daughter of a small farmer whose farm was at Wellpritton, just outside Holne, on Dartmoor. Before marrying, my grandmother-to-be had been in service in Torquay and she always remained loyal to the idea of contented subservience. She was a King and Country tory who thought any questioning of the 'right order of things' not merely dangerous but immoral.

Not so my grandfather. He probably voted whig, and he had a laughing disregard for all forms of kow-towing to those who assumed that they were his betters. As a young man he played football for Torquay United, an activity he had to give up because his bride wouldn't allow her husband to be associated with anything so vulgar as professional football. Some time after their marriage, which took place in the early years of the twentieth century, he went off to America to see if he could make a life for his family and himself there, but with the coming of war in 1914 he returned, volunteered for the army, fought at Gallipoli, was severely enough wounded to be invalided out, and in later years made a living as a supplier of cutlery and glassware to hotels and restaurants around the Torquay area.

It may have been his various experiences as thwarted footballer, unsuccessful adventurer, and wounded soldier, which gave my grandfather, whom I adored, a more quizzical view of history — local as well as national — than was common among men of his class. At all events, when I was a small boy he would tell me a good deal about Torquay's less than idyllic past. His stories fascinated me, especially one about how the town nearly burnt down 'years ago'. Years later, when I was beginning to work on the Life and Writings of a minor 19th century writer, W.H. Mallock, whose family came from Cockington Court, my grandfather gave me his copy of *The History of Torquay,* by J.T. White, printed, so the title page informs us, in Torquay, 'At the "Directory" Office. 1878'.

The same J.T. White had in 1850 produced the famous *Survey of Devon,* a formidably well-informed historical work which traces among much else the histories of the county's towns and villages, its geology and geography, and the genealogies of families, poor as well as rich. White is a man to be trusted. He is an example of that very recognisable breed of local historian, one which seems if not unique to the UK then uniquely prized. As is typical of its genre, White's *History of Torquay* draws on information provided, in White's own words, from 'the works of old and modern historians, manuscripts and deeds, charters and court rolls, the records of the State Office, and likewise the Reports of the Historical Manuscript Commissioners. In addition, the parish books, the parish registers, the churchwardens' book, the minute books of the Select Vestry, the Improvement Commissioners, and of the Torquay Local Board of Health, private letters, and the files of local newspapers, have been laid under contribution. Besides this, from a long residence in Torquay, I have been able to obtain a considerable amount of oral testimony from old inhabitants.' If White says it happened, it happened.

II

Brunel's railway line from London down to the west country was a great engineering feat of the 1830s. But it did not take in Torbay. That line, constructed after plans for an atmospheric railway had been tried and abandoned, opened in 1859. Before then, passengers for the bay area had been required to leave the train at Newton Abbot and make the rest of the journey by coach. Now they could alight at Torquay station or go onto Paignton. Citizens of both towns agreed that the coming of the railway age to Torbay deserved to be celebrated. But how? Local dignitaries combined with directors of the Dartmouth and Torbay Railway Company, who had raised the money for the line's construction, in deciding 'to feast the poor and make a monster pudding'.

Paignton had a history of creating puddings for the poor. The weight of the one made in 1819 had, so records insisted, amounted to 900lbs, and among its ingredients were 400lbs of flour, 120lbs of suet, 120lbs of raisins, 'and a large number of eggs'. But, so history also records, the result was disappointing. Slow cooking had reduced the outer part to paste and the inside wasn't even warm. It was therefore decided to bake the pudding for 1859 in no fewer than eight sections, which would be put together once the cooking was complete. In toto this pudding was to consist of — and here I quote White — '573lbs of flour, 191lbs of bread, 382lbs of raisins, 191lbs of currants, 382lbs of suet, 320 lemons, 144 nutmegs, 95lbs of sugar, a quantity of eggs, and 360 quarts of milk; the cost was £45'. Nor was this all. According to the same source, 'there were provided 1,900lbs of meat, 1,900lbs of bread, and an unlimited supply of the staple product of the Paignton orchards — cider'. The recipients of this generosity were to be the poor of the local parishes as well as the navvies who had worked on the line, and their wives and families. All very well meaning.

Unfortunately, there was no happy outcome. On the day set aside for the celebrations, tables and chairs were set up on the town green, which had been roped off for the day, and as the invitees to the feast took their places a procession of horses and wagons approached: one bread wagon, two of meats, each drawn by three horses, and, at the rear, the great pudding, its parts now put together, and of such a weight that the wagon it rode on had to be drawn by eight horses. As tradition required for this sort of occasion, the diners were served by gentlemen, farmers, and tradesmen. People ate, people drank. All was boisterous good humour. Then came the pudding.

Or rather, it didn't. The plan had been to cut the massive assemblage, its parts somehow bolted together, into hundreds of helpings and serve them once the dinner was over and done with. But the crowd which had been gathering on the edge of the green had other ideas. They had been growing increasingly restive at their exclusion from the feasting and drinking going on within the ring. Why couldn't they have their share, they wanted to know? Good question.

By one of history's necessary coincidences, that great *vade-mecum* of nineteenth-century literature, *Self-Help,* was first published in the same year that the outer world of Torbay (which is unlikely to have read Samuel Smiles's work) decided to help itself to the great pudding. Over the ropes they went and were soon surrounding the wagon on which stood five policemen trying to protect the pudding as well as the committee responsible for doling out the food. Fat chance. Soon, the intruders were taking matters and pudding into their own hands.

Then it got worse. 'Seeing the turn affairs were taking, the navvies and others at the tables, imagining that they were to be deprived of the toothsome delicacy, left their seats and swelled the tumultuous throng by whom the unfortunate pudding, committee, and policemen, were beleaguered.' White again, and though he goes on to describe the insurgents as a 'mob', you can tell his heart isn't in it. On the contrary, he's enjoying himself immensely. Toothsome delicacy, indeed. 'Alarmed at the menacing attitude of the crowd, the committee threw the pudding piecemeal at them... and this continued until not a morsel was left.' End of pudding.

III

Paignton's 'pudding riot' was a kind of carnivalesque. The world turned upside down. Bread riots were a different matter. During the latter 1840s they broke out all over England, including South Devon, and in 1847 there was a notable one in Torquay. This is understandable. There had been bad harvests in 1846 and again in 1847. Parish relief was barely able to cope with the distress of many living in and around the town. Despite this, 'over £600 was subscribed from private sources and church and chapel offertories' to help relieve the Irish famine. But then a letter from the Queen '"on behalf of the suffering Irish" was read in all the churches on the 21st April, 1847, and on Wednesday, the 24th March there was a general fast.' [White p. 168.] A fast for those whose tables are customarily groaning is one thing; it's quite another for those who are on parish relief. Bread riots began in Exeter in mid-May and soon spread to other Devon towns, including Torquay.

In recording this, White also notes that as the riot began at night, on Monday 17th May, there was difficulty in

94

identifying who the rioters were... 'Owing to the economy of the commissioners, no street lamps were permitted to be lit during the summer months, and to make matters worse, not only the lanterns but the burners had been removed .... With the view of identifying the ringleaders, it was determined to turn the gas on at the full; when this was done and the gas lit, each street lamp emitted a flame about a foot high, thoroughly illuminating the place.' Bread shops were broken open and bread chucked out, except where owners opened the shops of their own accord and 'the mob refrained from inflicting any damage'.

Nevertheless, there were arrests, and by midnight ten men were committed to Exeter gaol. Then something significant happens. The following day, at noon, 'a body of navvies, sixty in number, employed on the railway works above Torre ... marched into Torquay equipped with pick-axes, crowbars and shovels, with the avowed purpose of pulling down the Town Hall unless their fellow workers were liberated'.

They are eventually disarmed by a combination of police and coastguards, and by evening a detachment of forty men of the Fifth Fusiliers has arrived from Exeter to maintain law and order. To be on the safe side, 300 special constables are sworn in. [White p. 70]

The navvies who marched on Torquay in 1847 may not have succeeded in pulling down the Town Hall but their action does help to explain why a decade later the directors of the Dartmouth and Torbay Railway line were keen to reward them for their good work. It also explains another matter to which White alludes but whose significance he doesn't perhaps fully grasp. Twenty years later there was another substantial bread riot in Torquay. It occurred on 5th November, and I've no idea whether the date was especially chosen. Perhaps it was. After all, the 5th November used to be an occasion for bonfires and for burning effigies of hated figures. On this occasion, magistrates had apparently been warned there might be trouble. As a result 'one hundred special constables assembled at the Town Hall at eight o'clock; these were divided into detachments of thirty each, under the command of a leader and two subalterns, the whole being subject to the orders of the senior magistrate, Mr. March Phillips.'

It was Phillips who had read the Riot Act to the navvies in 1847 and then caused some of them to be committed to trial and prison. My guess is that memories died hard and that from the rioters' point of view Phillips was public enemy number one. At all events, he apparently decided against confrontation. 'No attempt was made to interfere with the men rolling tar barrels about the streets, so, emboldened by the passive action of the authorities, the mob set on some boys to attack the shop of a baker called Shinner ....' [Shinner is an old English name of what during the medieval period was commonly changed to Skinner — i.e. someone whose trade is skinning rabbit and other furs.]

What followed seems to have been a full-blown riot. Women brought up heavy stones which where thrown both at the constables and March Phillips. Phillips, who seems to have been singled out for especially rough treatment, was struck 'with such violence that one side of his face was greatly disfigured'. If he had been trying to mollify the rioters, it wasn't enough to save him. More looting, more smashing of windows, further attacks on bakeries.

Nor was that all. 'A diabolical attempt to plunge the town in darkness during the night was discovered just in time to avert what would no doubt have resulted in a serious calamity. A labourer named Chudleigh, with others, proceeded to Livermead, and there opened the road with the deliberate intention of severing the gas mains. He was arrested, and people at the gas works kept watch and ward over the threatened danger.' Who can blame them? Chudleigh's actions could have led to an almighty explosion.

But how explain this riot? White begins his next paragraph, 'This year, the conduct of the Fenian agitators inspired alarm throughout the country, and the local authorities obtained the sanction of Government to take measures for guarding against a disturbance'. But apparently nothing untoward happened, and 'in the following April the services of the special constables [three hundred had been sworn in] were dispensed with'. [White pp. 276-8].

White may be implying that Torquay's 1867 riot was fomented by Irish navvies. But Chudleigh is a good old Devon name, and it's not clear why there would still have been many navvies left in town once the railway was built. What is clear is that White views both bread riots as much more serious disturbances than the pudding riot. Property is involved, people are hurt, and of course had the plan to sever the gas main succeeded, Torquay might well have gone up in flames. As to why Chudleigh acted as he did, the explanation is surely that he was trying to prevent light from the gas lamps being used to identify the rioters. But this must mean that the riot was organised by locals. For you can only identify those you recognise. I doubt, in other words, that Fenian agitators had anything to do with the riot of 5th November, 1867. Still, it's a good way to deflect suspicion from home-grown agitators — a new under-class — who by the late 1860s would have had growing cause to resent the enrichment of hoteliers and shopkeepers of a superior kind as the railway brought increasing numbers of wealthy holiday-makers, just as they almost certainly resented the new class of resident settling along the English Riviera.

My father was born in Torquay. My mother's family came from Babbacombe, a village above Torquay. I myself was born in Excter. Until I read White's *History* I could see no particular reason to feel proud of my roots. It's different now.

The Mapping of Surnames
David McKie

One of the pleasures of browsing in graveyards is discovering the predominant names of those who are buried there. Sometimes they are names you might not expect to find in any profusion: a plethora of Pleydell-Bouveries, for instance; a cluster of Clutterbucks. Elsewhere one name may come close to monopoly status. Outside the disused church of St Columba, now a museum, at Bettyhill on the north coast of Scotland, there's something quite close to a full house of Mackays; the odd Munro and Macleod must feel like an interloper. More characteristic, though no less alluring, is the churchyard at a sweet little place called Arthuret, close to Longtown on the English side of the border with Scotland. Here you will find memorials to the Bells and Armstrongs and Littles who for centuries dominated life in this part of the land, but above all, the graves of the Grahams, whose uncompromising ascendancy no other family here could match. Reforming authority at one point packed large numbers of them off to Ireland, but they soon seeped back into their native territory, often masquerading under the name Maharg.

There used in my distant youth to be well understood rules in such matters. In England, by far the most dominant name was Smith, which seemed simple enough when so many earned their livings by smithing — blacksmiths, whitesmiths, goldsmiths, silversmiths and the like. The Smiths of Scotland were said to be its copious Robertsons, though I used to wonder at the philoprogenitive tendencies which that implied in men with the forename Robert. Family names in Wales almost always ended in S: if you weren't a Davis, Williams, or Jenkins, that was no doubt because you'd been born a Jones. (I once saw a British film comedy in which crowds were seen converging on Paddington station on the day of a rugby match at Twickenham. 'Would Mr David Jones from Wales please come to the stationmaster's office', the station announcer intoned; whereupon the entire assembly turned in its tracks to respond to the summons.) It was only while researching the Grahams of Arthuret, however, that I came across a far more sophisticated way of plotting who comes from where.

My guide in this exploration was a website called Public Profiler based on work at University College, London, which plots surnames across the world. If I tap in 'McKie' it uncovers a wealth of British McKies (on the map, they are coloured bright blue: the bluer an area looks, the more numerous your namesakes will be); an Australian contingent that's a little less blue, and lesser but still substantial presences in North America and more so, Canada. There are maps for 1881 and 1998, allowing one to discover the places people have left and where they have moved to. Both show British McKies as most prolific in Dumfries and Galloway. In 1881, England looks mercifully free from us, but a century later we've assembled in significant quantities, goodness knows why, in Hull and Hereford. The Grahams are bluest in far Australia, which may make those who read about them in George MacDonald Fraser's *The Steel Bonnets: the Story of the Anglo-Scottish Border Reivers* begin to ponder on transportation. Within the UK, they are strongest in Northern Ireland; within England, around Carlisle, the area in which Arthuret lies. In both 1881 and 1998 the border lands are replete with Grahams. The postal area there with the highest population of Grahams is Beckermet, near Egremont in West Cumbria.

The Smiths, to one of whom I am married (her mother was a Graham) are, as one would expect, the single most populous group in Great Britain, in 1998 as they were in 1881; thick on the ground in England, less so in Scotland except in the corner round Aberdeen, and surprisingly rare in Wales. The Joneses come second, concentrated in Wales and its eastern border; in London they are strongest in the north east sector round Romford, but compared with the 1881 picture seem to be on the retreat in the south east segment. Williamses, rather to my surprise, are shown in third place nationally, beating Browns into fourth.

I couldn't find any Pleydell-Bouveries. An aristocratic family of this name crops up a lot in the history of Swindon, but their numbers across the land are too sparse to get them into these maps — which no doubt they'd be very pleased about: so satisfying to be so exclusive. But Clutterbucks are a different matter. Their main area of congregation in both the late 19th century and the late 20th was Gloucester, spilling over into Bath and Bristol. Maybe some diligent Clutterbuck knows why in 1881 their main area of occupation in London was Croydon, but in 1998, that had switched to Harrow and Kingston. Public Profiler can tell you a lot, but it cannot answer a question like that.

I worry about the Clutterbucks, though. Their rate of occurrence per million names has declined from 38 in 1881 to 30 in 1998, reducing them in rank order from 3,873rd. to 4,777th. Come on, you Clutterbucks: do you want that trend to continue? True, as they might point out, the UCL evidence is not wholly incontrovertible; it's just the best you can do with a less than perfectly comprehensive database. Beware, even so: once you've accessed these maps (http://gbnames.publicprofiler.org) it may be quite some time before you do anything else.

'The Way to the Past':
Eavan Boland's Remapping of Irish History
Deirdre O'Byrne

'The way to the past is never smooth'
Eavan Boland

Eavan Boland's poem 'That the Science of Cartography is Limited' makes big claims for poetry, setting out to prove, as one might a problem of logic or mathematics, that it is a more accurate and complete rendering of the past than any geographical survey can be. The status of cartography is particularly questionable in the case of Ireland, where the mapping was an act of colonisation in itself, as is made clear in Brian Friel's *Translations*. The Ordnance Survey of Ireland was carried on right through the 1840s, the decade of the Irish Famine, and Boland links both historical events in this poem. Here, as is common in her work, Boland seeks to reclaim and record places which have been, not just overlooked, but deliberately elided by the cartographic procedure.

Eavan Boland's body of work is a kind of recovery process, and 'That the Science of Cartography is Limited' is a signature tune to her poetic project. She sets this out explicitly in 'The Journey', which plays with grand poetic traditions; as its preface suggests, it draws on the influence of classical Greek and Roman poetry. Perhaps more significantly, it subverts the Aisling dream-vision poems of ancient Irish literature, which feature a male narrator who is visited by a visionary female, calling on him for help in liberating her from bondage. According to the argument put forward by Boland in her polemical essay *A Kind of Scar*, the bondage for women is the actual patriarchal poetic tradition itself, which cast women as objects while denying their poetic voice. As befits one whose middle name is Aisling, Boland defies this gagging order and delineates her own poetic vision ('aisling' is the Gaelic for 'vision'). In the dream sequence of 'The Journey', Sappho appears to the poet, telling her: 'you are dear // and stand beside me as my own daughter'. As Virginia Woolf asserts in *A Room of One's Own*, women writers need their literary foremothers, and in 'The Journey', Boland acknowledges this need and claims her birthright as daughter of Sappho, while expressing her wish to 'at least be [a] witness' to the silenced, the unmapped, the disregarded. Sappho tells the poet in 'The Journey' to 'Behold the children of the plague', and a recurring feature of Boland's poetry is the fevered, starved and perishing populace who experienced the Irish Famine.

Boland's poetry has been criticised for being overly concerned with the domestic and the suburban, but much of her output is highly literary in its allusiveness. 'The Famine Road', for instance, contains a bitterly ironic tone that recalls the savage satire of Jonathan Swift. The poem also has biblical echoes; the voices of Lord Trevelyan and Colonel Jones in the epistolary passages are old-Testament-style in their cold-bloodedness, reminding us that Trevelyan saw the Irish Famine as an act of God to subdue a querulous nation. The Book of Ezekiel foretells that: 'A third part of you shall die of pestilence and be consumed with famine'. Ezekiel also prophesises that 'great hailstones will fall', which Boland seems to echo in her poem, in the unseasonable 'April hailstones' pelting the labourers. Similarly, Ezekiel's prognosis that 'fathers shall eat their sons in your midst, and sons shall eat their fathers' foreshadows Boland's famished workers each 'eye[ing] ... the other's buttock'.

The poem portrays precisely how the governing bodies conceive of the starving peasants as 'other': vampiric, cannibalistic, and sub-human. The third stanza begins by describing them as 'Sick, directionless'. As well as being a comment on their useless labour in constructing a road that leads nowhere, and their purposeless existence, these adjectives act as a judgement passed on these wretched people by their oppressors, who see them as morally sick, in fact, auto-vampiric: 'could they not blood their knuckles on rock'? The callousness of this rhetorical question is enforced by the hard consonance of 'knuckles', 'rock, suck', echoing the 'sick', 'fork, stick' of the first line of the stanza and echoed in turn in the final word of the stanza: 'buttock'. Furthermore, in the similarity of the four-lettered one-syllable form – sick, fork, rock, suck – the vocabulary calls up our most common expletive, as if the poet is nudging us, the readers, to curse in shock at the inhumane attitudes being expressed.

These starving people are regarded as willing to devour, not just their own flesh, but that of their comrades:

cunning as housewives, each eyed —
as if at a corner butcher — the other's buttock.

The poem, in its ironic portrayal of the famished people as would-be cannibals, recalls the satire of Jonathan Swift's *Modest Proposal* that the babies of Irish peasants be sold as a delicacy for the rich man's table. Swift published his proposal anonymously in 1729, commenting even then that Irish tenants were 'dying and rotting by cold and famine'. The subsequent century was to prove that his satire was as accurate as it was ineffectual. Bram Stoker, author of *Dracula* (1897), and the man who made vampires the stuff of popular culture, was Anglo-Irish, like Swift, and may also have been inspired by the writer's observation of the Irish scene. Stoker's novel appeared half-a-century after the Famine, but his tale of a decadent blood-sucking aristocrat preying on the surrounding peasantry, who stave him off with crucifixes, is analogous to the relationship between the worst of the exploitative landlords and their tenants. Part-vampire, part-cannibal, the road-builders in Boland's poem are

105

also allied to a fairy world; if they fail to gain sustenance from their own bodies or each other, they can exist without mortal food, by 'suck[ing] / April hailstones for water and for food'. The poet thus portrays the multi-faceted prejudices which deny the Irish peasants their humanity, a mechanism which enables those in power to deprive them of the most basic of human rights: food, and consequently, life.

In framing this portrayal of the Irish between the callous commentary of Trevelyan and Jones, Boland suggests that dehumanisation is happening on more than one level. If the colonisers regard the Irish as subhuman, this in turn dehumanises those in power, making them as cold-hearted as the snow and hail. Trevelyan can order Jones to

'give them no coins at all; their bones
need toil, their characters no less'.

Jones can respond in equally frigid terms:

'This Tuesday I saw bones
out of my carriage window.'

As a direct result of their mistreatment, the starved are losing their basic human instincts, 'walk[ing] clear' from a fellow-worker who 'has become / a typhoid pariah'. Even though the ailing man is related to a number of them, and 'shares [his blood] with some there', privation has turned their hearts as cold as the climactic conditions, and the customary practices of their culture appear to be collapsing:

No more than snow
attends its own flakes where they settle
and melt, will they pray by his death rattle.

The poem is thus making explicit that colonisation brutalises both colonisers and the colonised.

The mention of snow in 'The Famine Road' anonymises and depersonalises the sufferers, whose deaths are as common and unremarkable as the fall of a snowflake. In the italicised tercets which are interwoven with the stanzas concerning the famine, however, we are given a personal story. In the first three tercets, we hear the voice of a medical professional informing a woman that she is barren due to *'Anything ... spores,/a childhood accident'*. The cold detachment of the informant echoes that of Trevelyan and Jones, aligning the suffering woman with the starving road-builders; like them, she has no prospects. In the naming of one of the causes as *'spores'*, her infertility is linked to the spores which caused the blight of the potato crop. However, as extreme lack of food can cause infertility, the poem leads back again to the main cause of the barrenness: the fact that people are starved even though there are resources in the country. Because Trevelyan believed in free trade, he refused to prevent the export of corn from Ireland. As Jones in Boland's poem reports: 'we march the corn / to the ships in peace' because the wretched peasants are too ill to protest.

The narrator addresses the woman directly, in the final stanza, to empathise with her situation:

'Barren, never to know the load
of his child in you, what is your body
now if not a famine road?'

By presenting the story of one particular person as recipient of cold officialdom, Boland combats the authority figures who see them as undifferentiated as hailstones or snowflakes. Her sympathetic narrator provides a counterpoint to callousness.

In 'That the Science of Cartography is Limited', Boland also defies the objectification of the poor. As defence against the icily dominant voices of the counterparts of Trevelyan and Jones, she provides an intimate moment between lovers, while rejecting any stereotypes of traditional love poetry. The opening of the poem has the register of a mathematical theorem, setting forth 'what I wish to prove'. It then abruptly changes key for the second stanza:

> When you and I were first in love we drove
> to the borders of Connacht
> and entered a wood there.

For an Irish reader, this has echoes of Cromwell's infamous edict which sent displaced peasants 'to hell or to Connaught', suggesting that the narrator and her lover are following in the footsteps of other migrants. 'When you and I were first in love' has the sing-song quality of the opening line of a ballad, and the part-rhyme of 'love' and 'drove' enhances the lyrical feel, but they also form part-rhymes for 'prove' in the first stanza, so, though we seem to have moved into the realms of romantic verse, we are not allowed to forget that this poem has a didactic purpose. Like protagonists of a fairy story, the lovers 'entered a wood', but as in most folktales, which, after all, are equally instructive, something unsettling is hidden in the undergrowth:

> Look down you said: this was once a famine road.

Just as the famine roads themselves tend to end abruptly, in woods, bogs or on mountainsides, this line is placed on its own, with no supporting or following lines to form a stanza.

Boland, with an avowed interest in oral history, gives storytelling a key role in this poem. The poet is at once the listener and the mediator of her partner's story:

> I looked down ... as you told me
> in the second winter of their ordeal, in
>
> 1847, when the crop had failed twice,
> Relief Committees gave
> the starving Irish such roads to build.

She hears the tale and passes it on through the medium of this poem, thus writing herself and her partner into the pattern of Irish history; if maps do not record this road, they will. The 'you' in the story becomes the historian, and the poet takes up that baton in her turn. The onus is thus on the reader in turn to pass on the story. The poem tells us that:

> Where they died, there the road ended
> and ends still

but, she is adamant, it is not where their story ends. By commemorating them in poetry, she is making the same claims for the immortality of verse as Shakespeare does in his sonnets. In Sonnet 55, he refers to the 'unswept stone besmear'd with sluttish time', as Boland writes of 'rough-cast stone' disappearing under 'ivy and the scutch grass'. Both poets are promising that their lines can outlast mere stonework. In official Irish maps, the 'line' of the famine road is unrecorded, just as the lineage of the road-builders is unknown, lost, buried, or unborn. Like the longed-for child of the barren woman in 'The Famine Road', it will not exist:

> the line which says woodland and cries hunger
> and gives out among sweet pine and cypress

> will not be there.

Following the pattern of the one-line stanza in which the narrator is first told to look down at the famine road, the poem's final four words are left on their own, declaiming in staccato that they

> *will not be there.*

The implicit claim, though, is that her lines of poetry *will* be there. The narrator is reiterative; she 'take[s] down / the map of this island' to tell herself 'again' that the famine road is unchronicled. But in the sense that to 'take down' can also mean to lower someone else's status (as in to take down a peg or two), she is returning to the theorem of her first stanza, undermining the hierarchy of the allegedly 'masterful' map-makers and their ability to create a true record. The 'line' which 'gives out' doesn't just document that it expires, or gives up; Hiberno-Irish lends it ambiguity. The idiomatic use of 'give out' is difficult to translate into standard English, but the nearest meaning is to complain or chastise. Therefore, if we read with Irish idiom in mind, the line of the famine road, like the line of Boland's poetry, remains there as an endless reproach.

The poem 'Quarantine' continues the process of combatting de-individualisation by presenting one particular couple who died in the famine, against the backdrop of the unknown numbers who perished or emigrated. Once again, the poem has echoes of myth:

> In the worst hour of the worst season
> of the worst year of a whole people.

The repetition and rhythm suggest folk narrative. These opening lines set up a large canvas, but then the poem moves sharply into focus on 'a man [who] set out from the workhouse with his wife'. One might assume that leaving the workhouse would mean a move to a better place, except that, as many workhouses at the time of the Irish Famine were overcrowded and underfunded, they were rife with disease. There are echoes in this opening stanza of the biblical Mary and Joseph: a couple travelling 'In the worst hour of the worst season/ of the worst year', at night 'under freezing stars'. However, there is no donkey to carry the woman in this tale; the narrator interjects a reminder '– they were both walking –'. The only creature available to carry the woman is the man himself:

> She was sick with famine fever and could not keep up.
> He lifted her and put her on his back.

Neither is there a miraculous ending to this tale; it ends with death, not a saviour's birth. As in 'The Famine Road', the resonant set-up is undercut with bald statement:

110

In the morning they were both found dead.
Of cold. Of hunger. Of the toxins of a whole history.

The poem's focus moves out once again, from the dead couple at the centre to the 'whole history' of a people. They become emblematic of the sufferings of their nation under colonialism. But then we're brought back to the personal intimate relationship between these two:

> her feet were held against his breastbone.
> The last heat of his flesh was his last gift to her.

How inadequate are the gold, frankincense, myrrh or routine red roses of religious or traditional love narratives compared to the last heat of an ebbing life.

The poem 'Quarantine' appears in a sequence titled 'Marriage' in Code (2001). In the second part of that sequence, Boland pronounces on the inadequateness of romantic verse: 'Love poetry can do no justice to this'. She illustrates this in the poem 'Quarantine'; no love-language is capable of recording such an event. The imperative fourth stanza forbids sentimentality or lyricism:

> Let no love poem ever come to this threshold.
> There is no place here for the inexact
> praise of the easy graces and sensuality of the body.

As readers, we must agree. To speak of 'easy graces and sensuality' in such a context would be obscene. As the poem says: 'There is only time for this merciless inventory'. We are required, in reading this poem, to bear witness alongside the poet. The inventory of the five chopped phrases of the final stanza catalogues what we need to recall:

> Their death together in the winter of 1847.
> Also what they suffered. How they lived.
> And what there is between a man and woman.
> And in which darkness it can best be proved.

111

Famine road above Killary Harbour
© Copyright Graham Horn (Creative Commons Licence)

As in 'That the Science of Cartography is Limited', the poet sets out to prove something in a poem, claiming equal, or rather higher, status for poetry compared to mathematical operation or scientific experiment.

Boland's theory that poetry is the device of choice for chronicling such an unspeakable atrocity as the Irish Famine has been proven in recent history, in the unlikely sites of football arenas. The poetry in question is a ballad, 'The Fields of Athenry', which tells the story of a young man who is deported, leaving wife and child, because he 'stole Trevelyan's corn'. The song has become ubiquitous at Irish football and rugby matches, and is equally popular with the Irish diaspora, obviously tapping into a need to remember the forgotten, to sing of the unknown. Like the song, which is widely believed to be a traditional folksong though it was actually written by Dubliner Pete St John in the 1970s, Boland's poetry evokes and embeds folk narratives in ways which resonate with contemporary audiences.

Her poems speak with a voice which is defiantly female and defiantly Irish. I have referred above to Boland's use of folk narrative, oral tradition and Irish idiom. In the poem 'An Irish Childhood in England: 1951', we read of

> the teacher in the London convent who
> when I produced "I amn't" in the classroom
> turned and said – "you're not in Ireland now".

Her famine poems are the answer to that. The Irish child in England who 'didn't know what to hold, to keep' has now discovered what she needs to cherish, and the adult poet speaks assertively back to that silencing voice to say: I *am* in Ireland now.

Boland, Eavan, *A Kind of Scar: The Woman Poet in a National Tradition*, Dublin: Attic, 1989
Boland, Eavan, 'An Irish Childhood in England', 'Quarantine', 'That the Science of Cartography is Limited', 'The Famine Road', 'The Journey', in *New Collected Poems*, Manchester: Carcanet, 2005
Friel, Brian, *Translations*, London: Faber, 1981
St John, Pete, 'The Fields of Athenry', http://www.petestjohn.com/works/the-fields-of-athenry/ (official website of Pete St John)
Stoker, Bram, *Dracula*, London: Penguin, 2003. First published 1897.
Swift, Jonathan, *A Modest Proposal and other Satirical Works*, New York: Dover, 1996. First published 1729
Woolf, Virginia, *A Room of One's Own*, London: Penguin, 2000. First published 1929

'An Expensive Death':
Walter Benjamin at Portbou
John Payne

No-one goes to Portbou unless they have to. Perched above the last bay on the Spanish side of the border with France, it is dominated by its railway station and marshalling yards. But these days most visitors to Catalonia (now an autonomous region of Spain) arrive by aeroplane or use the motorway crossing ten miles inland.

In 1940 everything was different. Walter Benjamin arrived on foot, in a small party led by Lisa Fitkko. Setting out from the little French Catalan holiday resort of Banyuls-sur-Mer, they had had climbed inland over the foothills of the Pyrenees before descending into the bay of Portbou. A couple of years before, Stephen Spender had described it in his poem 'Port Bou' as like a child clutching a favourite pet, the arms not quite meeting around the animal's body. That is how it is today, how it was in 1940.

Benjamin had an entry visa for the USA. He had a transit visa for Spain and Portugal. But he did not have an exit visa for France, half of it occupied by the Nazis, half of it on loan to the collaborationist Vichy regime. He was a sick man, with a heart condition, and the trek across the mountains must have been a fresh torture for him. Some say he was carrying an important manuscript with him. We do not know.

It is dangerous to argue from an author's writing to an author's life. But that overwhelmingly powerful figure of the 'Angel of History', carried forward on the gale, her face turned to the past, observing the destruction in her wake, haunts me. Perhaps more than anything, more than Picasso's 'Guernica', Alain Resnais' 'Night and Fog',

Scale: 0 10 20 30 km

Legend:
- ·—·—· International boundary
- △ Mountains
- ● Monastery
- ▢ Greco-Roman remains

FRANCE

△ CANIGÓ

Collioure ●
Port Vendres ●
Banyuls ●
La Jonquera ●
Portbou ●
Colera ●
El Port de la Selva ●
Sant Pere de Rodes ●
Cadaqués ●
CAP DE CREUS
Vilabertran ●
Figueres ●
Castelló d' Empúries ●
Roses ●
EMPORDÀ
Besalú ●
Aiguamolls de L'Empordà Natural Park
GARROTXA
Olot ●
Fluvià
Empúries ▢
L'Escala ●
△ FINESTRES
△ ROCACORBA
Ter
L'Estartit ●
Islas Medes Natural Park
Brugent
Llémena
Ter
◉ GIRONA
Peratallada ●
Pals ●
La Bisbal ●
Begur ●
Aiguablava
Ter
● Sant Hilari Sacalm
△ SERRA DE MONTSENY
Sant Feliu de Guíxols ●
C O S T A   B R A V A
Tossa ●
Lloret ●
Blanes ●
MEDITERRANEAN SEA
Barcelona ↙

GIRONA AND THE COSTA BRAVA

Map courtesy of Mary Mackenzie

it summarises the savaging of people's lives by the forces let loose in the twentieth century: the corrosive links between technology, xenophobia and authoritarian politics. The twentieth century was about the need to be right, to possess the truth, while other values — fairness, kindness, nurture — were dismissed as only relevant for the weak of the earth.

There is remembering, and there is forgetting. Somewhere in an individual life, and somewhere in the collective life of a community or a society, a balance must be struck. To go to Portbou now is to remember, to question, and then perhaps allow the past to become what it should be — the past — rather than a haunting, obsessive dream that we seek to deny but cannot. That is perhaps what the Spanish novelist Javier Cercas thought when he visited Portbou in 1998. He was working on his novel *Soldados de Salamina* (2001; translated into English as *Soldiers of Salamis*) which is about forgetting and remembering too. A lot had been forgotten since the end of the Franco regime, he told me in an interview in 2002, perhaps too much. Paraphrasing George Santayana, he suggested that a nation (Spain? Catalonia? probably both) that has not come to terms with its past is in danger of repeating it.

Cercas was not alone in thinking this. A growing social movement in Spain has attempted to recover individual and social memory in relation to family members, friends and neighbours who died either during the Civil War or in the harsh repression of the Franco years. This led to the passing of a new law in 2007, known as the Law of Historical Memory, which paves the way to the official opening of common war-graves (there are 179 in Catalonia alone), for appeals against arbitrary military tribunal verdicts (110,000 of these in Catalonia in the aftermath of the war) and the removal at long last of remaining Franquist symbols from public buildings. Finally, it seems, there is an official shift from the years of transition to a definitive break with the past.

The cemetery, Benjamin's cemetery, is on one of the arms of the bay, on cliffs sloping first gently, then precipitously, towards the sea. You can see the empty Customs House on the opposite cliff, where the road climbs anxiously towards France. But we are all Europeans now, so... In the opposite direction, descending the hill towards Portbou, the cemetery is there, laid out in plan view, on the sloping cliffs. Bathing early, in one of the south-facing coves, and there is the cemetery again. There are brooding clouds over the Pyrenees, a heavy, groaning swell in the bay. Both mountains and sea speak of eternity, both mountains and sea change constantly. Perhaps that is why Javier Cercas said that hope too is infinite. It is so hard to live in the present moment, and in its truth.

In 1979, soon after the transition to democracy in Spain, the locals clubbed together for a monument to Benjamin, at the spot where his body was taken from its niche in 1945 and thrown into the common grave. Some years later, the official monument was built — designed by the Israeli artist Dani Karavan, and paid for (eventually) by the German government. Lisa Fitkko attended the inauguration in 1994. A metal staircase disappears steeply into the cliffs. Seventy steps down, it is filled with a glass panel, initially reflecting the image of the person descending, but then opening onto a view of water churning upon rocks far below. The steps continue, the steps we fear, the steps we know we shall all have to take one day, to the gaschamber or the firing-squad, or just to nothingness and oblivion. The eighty-eighth step marks the final leap into the unknown.

The words engraved on the glass panel — in German, English, Spanish and Catalan — remind us of another of Benjamin's thoughts: 'It is more arduous to honour the memory of the nameless than that of the renowned. Historical construction is devoted to the memory of the nameless.' Benjamin is a name, but Karavan has sought to remember at Portbou all those who died and continue to die because of their race, their religion, their ideas, the mere accident of being the wrong person in the wrong place at the wrong moment.

But it is not my moment yet. Returning up the steps, I read on the townspeople's memorial more words by Benjamin: 'There is no document of civilisation that cannot also become a document of barbarism.' That short, terrible twentieth century again. In the cemetery is the niche of my friend's grandfather Lluís Cabré Ycart. I knew him and liked him. He lived longer than the short century — from 1902 until 2000, long enough to see hope, not long enough to see his hopes dashed by a new century that seems determined to repeat the crimes of the old one.

Photo by Sandra Payne

Dani Karavan monument

Karavan made it clear that his monument is not just related to those driven from their homes between 1933 and 1945, but that it represents both a naming of the victims and a call for tolerance and understanding in the future. In Spain, they are beginning to remember the long co-existence of Christian, Jewish and Muslim communities during the Middle Ages. In 1986, King Juan Carlos could not quite bring himself to call the religious building in the heart of Cordoba a mosque. But he did announce that 'The light that shines upon us from the cathedral at Cordoba is in no way faint or trembling. It is intense and penetrating. It lights up our pathway. It suggests the growing together of the world's communities.' That was something to be thankful for after that short, terrible twentieth century.

119

The mystery of Benjamin's death, on the night of 25/26 September 1940, lingers on. The decision to move his remains to a common grave in 1945 may have simply been because there was no-one to pay for the upkeep of his niche in the Catholic section of the cemetery. Equally, in the delicate circumstances of a fascist state (Spain) hoping to survive into a post-fascist world, there may have been evidence to hide. To our shame, of course, Franco's Spain survived for thirty years.

Hannah Arendt, who did so much to keep the memory of Benjamin and his writings alive, came here in October 1940. Looking for what? A manuscript, or something else? Those who accompanied Benjamin across the Pyrenees were allowed to continue on their way. Why, if Benjamin was so convinced that they were about to be returned to France that he committed suicide, were they allowed to continue their journey?

As for the suicide, we know that Benjamin had experimented with consciousness-altering drugs on the island of Ibiza in 1932. We know that he regularly took morphine in relation to a heart condition. At least three possibilities remain: suicide (which may have been despair at the state of Europe, or personal despair at the prospect of being sent back to France); an accidental overdose; a political murder, perhaps by Nazi agents collaborating with Franco's police.

The cost of Benjamin's death was considerable. We know this because the documents have survived. So much for the coffin, so much to the hotel for use of a room by the undertaker. The hotel bill has survived too. So who did Walter Benjamin call on the night before his death, phone-calls that cost almost as much as the room itself? Phone-calls that were almost certainly not to Spain? Elaine Feinstein's novel *The Border* is of little help, fine as it is. Like Javier Cercas, she wrote of forgetting and of remembering, but Benjamin himself remains only a shadowy background figure, even if aspects of the fictional characters bear more or less resemblance to Benjamin's life in 1930s Europe. Feinstein seemed convinced of the suicide, even referring to 'the logic of his decision'.

Remembering and forgetting. Perhaps it is time to let the bones of Walter Benjamin lie peacefully. After all, we have his writings, which is all a writer should ever wish to be remembered by. Better to turn our attention from an imperfect past to an imperfect present. From Portbou, on a glorious evening full of sun and shooting vines and gleaming hilltop castles, we drove to Collioure, the ancient seat of the Knights Templars. The border was no longer there, the customs closed, no barrier, no policeman. At a beachside café in France we paid for our beer with the same Euro notes and coins we had used a few hours before in Portbou.

And yet, and yet. As we returned south in the gloaming to Portbou, the doubts resurfaced. The Right is gathering strength again, not least in France and Spain. The borders may be open within Europe, but they remain largely closed to refugees and asylum-seekers from beyond Europe's borders. These nameless people include the bodies washed up every week on the shores of the Straits of Gibraltar, Africans trying in vain to escape tyranny, war and hatred and — the greatest oppression of all — poverty. What happened at Portbou is important to all of us. We all need to descend that staircase, confront our own mortality, confront the harm we do every day to one another and to our planet. The crimes that are committed by soldiers, police and bureaucrats — in our names.

We, who are not nameless.

A Short Walk Up Dere Street
Mark Patterson

*'The sun shone brightly out of a clear sky, giving a
sense of benediction, as I started upon my northward journey.'*

So began *Agricola's Road into Scotland*, written by the
Cornish artist Jessie Mothersole, published by The Bodley
Head in 1927. Mothersole was a suffragette, a painter of
pretty coastal scenes and an inveterate tramper of
Britain's Roman relics and her latest book recounted her
journey along most of the great Roman road Dere Street,
which ran from York to the Firth of Forth. Construction of
the road, which is studded with Roman forts and temporary military camps along its length, including its passage
through the lonely wilderness of the Cheviot hills in the
Borders, has long been attributed to the work of Roman
legionary soldiers in the late 1st century as they advanced
northward under the command of Gnaeus Julius Agricola.
This general, whose hagiographical biography by his son-
in-law Tacitus is one of the most valuable classical sources
on the Roman occupation of Britain, had been appointed
as governor of the province a few years into a recharged
campaign to complete the military domination of the
island. Agricola wasted no time in taking the war to the
province's remaining unconquered tribes in northern
England and Scotland and his troops advanced to the
Clyde-Forth line by 81. By 84 or 85 they had moved up the
east coast at least as far as the Moray Firth, building forts
and roads to service the new front. Dere Street was the
most important of these roads, constituting the main east
coast line of communication between the Empire's most
northerly frontier and the most northerly legionary base
at York.

Some 1900 years later it is inevitable that long stretches of the Roman road have disappeared — ploughed out, stone stolen, built over. Yet on balance more of the road is probably still usable or at least visible — in one form or another — than has been lost. Following its route today is to make both a great physical journey through two nations and a journey into the history of maps, both real and imagined.

Antiquarians and travellers such as John Leland, William Camden, John Horsley and William Stukeley all noted surviving parts of the great road or its attendant military installations while 20th century travellers after Mothersole included the *Daily Telegraph*'s irritable countryside columnist J.H.B. Peel, the popular archaeology writer Leonard Cottrell and the doyen of writers on Britain's Roman roads, Ivan D. Margary. These successive descriptions of Dere Street have created an accretion of commentary, built up by writers feeding off the commentary of previous writer, which tends to touch on two aspects of the road's lingering survival: they show how the physical remains of the Roman road have become increasingly obscure over the centuries, and they give us a related bigger picture of social change in Britain. In the 1920s, for example, the roads were so quiet that Jessie Mothersole was able to follow the entire length of Dere Street up to the Tweed on foot and bicycle in perfect safety. Her journey included cycling up the old Great North Road, which lay on top of Dere Street in north Yorkshire, to Scotch Corner, which remains a north-south and east-west junction today just as it was in Roman times. But by Ivan Margary's time in the 1950s old irregularities in the Great North Road here were being ironed out by the 'great dual-carriageway road' that had taken its place. Then, in the early 1970s, when J.H.B. Peel came this way in a car, driving at 35mph when all around him were doing 70, Scotch Corner was a 'screeching modern roundabout.' God knows what he would make of the traffic now.

Further north in County Durham, Mothersole, Peel and Leonard Cottrell (who only drove the road sections, so missing much of the Roman route) noted the bleak impact on the countryside of the county's coal mines and related heavy industries such as the vast steelworks at Consett. But that was then. The steelworks closed down in early 1981, making Consett a ghost town, while the relics of Durham coal mining have since been relegated to the role of an attraction in north east England's heritage industry.

Dere Street today is partly a living highway and partly the ghost of a road. In England the Roman route is followed by the modern A1 in Yorkshire as far as Scotch Corner as well as several minor and major highways in County Durham and Northumberland. In the Borders, the road remained in use as a track for Scottish cattle drovers into the 19th century but this section has now fallen out of use by traffic. In its obscure lengths Dere Street can often still be traced, with increasing difficulty, via country tracks, footpaths and field boundaries which follow its alignments. There are also several places where the high Roman road embankment still survives in subdued form, such as a farmer's field running north from Corbridge in Northumberland. This feature was described as being 'very perfect' by Henry MacLauchlan, who wrote a precise and valuable description of Dere Street between the Tees and the Scottish border in the 1850s when he was in the service of the Duke of Northumberland. Mothersole saw the same feature in the 1920s and I almost punched in the air in triumph when I saw the same low embankment running across the field during my own endeavour to walk Dere Street from York to its probable termination near Edinburgh. Hunting down Roman roads can have that effect on you.

Alternatively, you can follow Dere Street with the help of maps, since the road is clearly marked on the relevant modern, orange Ordnance Survey Explorers. Mothersole used an OS map in her own journey in the 1920s without specifying which one. She may have used the regular One-Inch maps which had Dere Street marked as 'Roman Road.' And she could have taken along the new OS *Map*

MacLauchlan saw it, Mothersole saw it... the raised mound of Dere Street running north from the Roman fort at Corbridge in Northumberland

of Roman Britain, which was published with huge popular success in 1924. The man responsible for this map, and its equally successful second edition in 1928, was O.G.S. Crawford, who had been taken on as the OS's first Archaeology Officer and given the task of thoroughly revising the service's mapping of antiquities. Until then, this aspect of the Ordnance Survey's work had been patchy and uneven, with the quality and thoroughness of antiquities mapping varying from county to county.

Despite these problems, the mapping of Dere Street itself can be dated back to the very origins of the Ordnance Survey in the 18th century following the pioneering work of the surveyor William Roy in Scotland. After the Hanoverian defeat of the Jacobite uprising at Culloden in 1746, Roy became part of a project to produce a detailed map of the whole of Scotland for the assistance of the British army... and to aid the eventual 'pacification' of the Highlands. George II's son, 'Butcher' Cumberland, was in overall charge of the task, which was to be carried out by an expert team including Roy as Assistant Quartermaster and the draughtsman Paul Sandby, the artist who went on to become an accomplished watercolourist and one of the founding artists of the Royal Academy. In 1755, after seven years' labour, the Great Map was complete and Roy, who had been a civilian during the survey, joined the army, seeing service in Europe where his work included making a plan of the Battle of Minden. But Roy also had abiding antiquarian interests and his mapping work in Scotland had brought him into contact with some of Scotland's surviving Roman fortifications.

This interest led to Roy's *Military Antiquities of the Romans in North Britain*, published posthumously in 1793 and still of great value because it included plans of Roman installations which are no longer in existence above ground. Roy's book includes an account of Dere Street's probable route and a small number of lovely topographical engravings of Dere Street in the Borders. A set of three plates, for example, shows the road where it passes a complex cluster of Roman training camps at Chew Green just before it passes over the border into Scotland from Coquetdale in Northumberland (these camps can all be seen today).

Another plate shows the route of the road near the large Roman camp of *Trimontium*, near Newstead at the foot of the Eildon Hills in Scotland. It was here, on the south bank of the Tweed, that Jessie Mothersole ended her journey, probably wisely since even the confident modern OS route for the Roman road becomes distinctly patchy north of this point. Yet, while Roy's surveying and drawing skills may have been superb, he was one of many learned people whose writings about Roman Britain became warped by one of the most outrageous scholarly hoaxes of the 18th century. The hoax was perpetrated by one Charles Bertram, an Englishman living in Copenhagen who claimed he had discovered a hitherto unknown 14th century transcript of a Roman document titled *De Situ Britanniae* concerning the geography and people of Roman Britain. Made by a monk called Richard of Cirencester, the manuscript, and an accompanying map, contained scores of Roman place names that were completely new to historians. The matter was a revelation to antiquarians such as William Stukeley, whom Bertram had first contacted and who indeed became the chief vehicle for the dissemination of the startling new information.

The map, the new place names and even Richard of Cirencester were all fictions devised by Bertram for reasons unknown. Some have suggested that it was a scholarly joke gone too far, or an elaborate way of Bertram attracting attention to himself. Whatever his motivation, Bertram's high quality forgery influenced thinking and writing on Roman Britain for several decades. His victims included William Roy, who wastefully devoted part of Book IV of *Military Antiquities of the Romans in North Britain* to an attempt to adjust existing knowledge of Roman Scotland to the hoax revelations of the medieval manuscript that Bertram sent to Stukeley in 1749.

Roy's initial account of Dere Street's route from Yorkshire into Scotland accorded very well with the route that is today marked on modern OS maps. Unfortunately, he then gave himself the task of trying to fit in new place names along the route, such as *Curia*, *Ad Fines* and *Praeturium*, which were all the products of Charles Bertram's imagination. Today such matters may read like curious historical footnotes, yet there is a fascination in the way that Dere Street connects such matters as the Jacobite rebellion, literary forgeries, cartography, 18th century painters and the founding of the Ordnance Survey in a cultural cascade of footnotes and footnotes-upon-the-footnotes that would have been familiar to the great antiquarians.

But following the great road can be physically exciting, and challenging, too. And on this score Mothersole, I

Entrance to a new housing development near Tow Law, County Durham

think, is the kind of woman whom the *Daily Mail* would get away with calling 'the indomitable Miss Mothersole', based on her feat of cycling and walking the entire route in all weather, and wading streams and shallow rivers when the need arose. One day she even risked being shelled by the British army. This occurred on a long, lonely stretch of Dere Street where it passed over the army's artillery ranges immediately north of the Roman fort of *Bremenium* in Northumberland. Mothersole records that she was allowed to travel along this road despite the fact that artillery practice with live ammunition was taking place that day. '...as we walked we could hear the shells whizzing over our heads and then the dull explosions in the distance,' she wrote. 'We could see rows of dummy men set up to be fired at, and the turf-covered dug-outs of the officers who were watching the effects of the shells. Farther on...we passed a dummy man lying in the grass among the shell-holes.' The ranges are now part of the British army's ninety square mile, 60,000-acre Otterburn training area. And while changes to army health and safety rules means you are now not allowed to enter the area when manoeuvres are taking place I was still firmly advised by a local historian not to walk off the road in case stray ordnance blew my leg off.

By the time Osbert Guy Stanhope Crawford was appointed as the Ordnance Survey's first Archaeology

Friendly warning sign next to Dere Street on the Otterburn army ranges

Officer in 1920, tasked with revising the service's mapping of Britain's antiquities, cartographers had a new tool at their service — air photography. During the Great War Crawford had worked as an air observer with the Royal Flying Corps and had flown daily reconnaissance missions in Bristol fighters where he took photographs and made precise records of enemy positions. After the war, and

with Crawford now the only civilian in a service dominated by military people, he used air photograpy in his
crusade to improve and standardise the OS's approach to
the inclusion of antiquities on its maps. To this end he
developed a close relationship with the RAF and used
images taken by its air photographers to improve the
identification of ancient features in the landscape that
were otherwise difficult or even impossible to see on the
ground. Meanwhile, Crawford also brought his own expert
eye to bear on the issue, riding far and wide on a specially
adapted bicycle to identify and record ancient features in
the landscape. This detailed fieldwork was complemented
by the work of a merry band of unpaid volunteers whom
Crawford referred to as his 'Honorary Correspondents',
helping Crawford to complete a county-by-county revision
of the plotting of historic and pre-historic features on OS
maps (Crawford's story, including his conversion to and
disillusionment with communism, is told by Kitty Hauser
in *Bloody Old Britain*, Granta). Out of this work Crawford
also devised the idea of creating popular 'Period Maps,' of
which the first, the *Map of Roman Britain,* sold its 1,000
print-run within a month of publication in August, 1924,
forcing a second run of 4,500 copies. The map, which
shows all known Roman towns, installations and roads, is
now in its fifth edition. But while each of the editions has
been slightly different from its predecessor, reflecting
changing archaeological knowledge, one constant is that
none of the Roman roads are named. This is a professional
admission that nobody knows what names the Roman
invaders gave their British roads, if they called them anything, and that the popular titles they have today — such
as Ermine Street, Watling Street, Fosse Way and Dere
Street — are tidy modern versions of names which probably originate with the Anglo-Saxons. The history of Dere
Street itself is further complicated by its long misidentifi-
cation with Watling Street, which is better known as the
Roman road which runs from Dover to Wroxeter in
Shropshire via London. Despite this, Dere Street was

named as Watling Street throughout the 19th century on maps such as the OS First Series, which also included occasional quaint antiquarian fancies such as a 'Druidical Circle' marked beside the road north of the Cheviots. The Watling error continued into the early 20th century and has left a permanent mark on various towns in north east England where residential Watling Terraces, Watling Roads and Watling Streets exist close to or on the route of the Roman road. The name swung back to its earlier title of Dere Street in the 20th century and this was the name used by Jessie Mothersole, who blamed the 18th century antiquarians for the Watling Street mistake. Although there is no agreement on the origin of the name Dere Street, consensus points to a connection with Deira, which was the southernmost of two linked regions within the Anglo-Saxon kingdom of Northumbria, which covered an area from the Firth of Forth down through Yorkshire. The

The Roman road runs this way... mis-named Watling Terrace in Willington, County Durham

name Dere Street was thus Anglo-Saxon recognition of the permanent paved road which ran up through their entire kingdom; a testimony to the endurance of Roman road building and surveying skills.

Where Mothersole may have gone wrong is in repeating the long-held belief that the ancient road was built by Agricola's soldiers. This doubt arises from a fresh batch of research that has taken place into the skills that were necessary to build long roads such as Dere Street. This, in turn, is a reminder that nobody actually knows how the Romans managed to build straight roads connecting locations that were many miles apart, with the equipment they had then. Several newly articulated theories about Roman surveying techniques are in circulation, one (argued by John Poulter in *The Planning of Roman Roads and Walls in Northern Britain*, Amberley) being that Dere Street was planned as several long alignments but that the road building itself may have taken place many years after the original survey. If Poulter is correct, the construction of the road occurred after Agricola was recalled to Rome in the mid '80s of the 1st century. Thus, Dere Street may not be *Agricola's Road into Scotland* after all. The other relevant idea for our purposes comes from Hugh Davies (*Roads in Roman Britain*, Tempus) who theorises that Roman roads were first planned on huge maps as part of detailed geographical surveys of the landscapes through which the roads were to be built. That none of these maps have survived is immaterial to his argument; Davies believes their most likely form would have been as temporary layouts on the floors of large rooms, with survey lines being marked, painted or scratched in sand on the floor. Thus, Dere Street, this ancient highway that pulls us north through landscape and time, could have originated in the most elementary kind of map known to humanity — a few lines drawn in the dirt.

Heading north... a solid stretch of Dere Street in the Scottish Borders looking towards Newton St Boswells, now used as a country track

Beyond Boundary Passage
Andrew Whitehead

Few alleys live up to their name as well as this one. Boundary Passage once gave precarious access to a concealed world. From the naptha lights, the stalls, the relative abundance of Shoreditch High Street, this stub of an isthmus — barely a speck in even the most compendious A-to-Z — was the entrance to the Old Nichol, one of late Victorian London's more ill-famed slums.

The passageway still has a hint of the sinister. The walls are high and grimy. It's studded with posts, apocryphally once cannons in Nelson's navy. Arthur Morrison would recognise the place. In his classic novel *A Child of the Jago*, he rechristened the alley as 'The Posties'. It is described in the opening page: 'off Shoreditch High Street, a narrow passage, set across with posts, gave menacing entrance' on the criminal slum he depicted. 'What was too vile for Kate Street, Seven Dials, and Ratcliff Highway in its worst day, what was too useless, incapable and corrupt — all that teemed in the Old Jago.' 'The Posties' was the route taken by slum boys lifting from the stalls and running for home ground — the path of more professional villains in search of a fence — the limits of where police would patrol other than in pairs. Both passage and boundary.

Morrison prefaced his novel with a street plan — a fictional but precise mapping of his 'Jago' on the lay-out of the Nichol. Only the names changed. So Boundary Street, at the inner end of the passage, became Edge Lane. Morrison sought to assert the truth of his account by this faithful rendition of its street map and the clear echo of the original in his street names. But the one has subsumed the other. The 'Jago' is now better known than the Nichol. There is, not far away on Great Eastern Street —

The map included in Arthur Morrison's 1896 novel A Child of the Jago

not quite in Morrison's catchment area — an up-market clothes joint entitled 'A Child of the Jago'. Cheekily, it has trademarked the name as what it calls a 'cult brand' and, as I write, has its 'Jago Navy Slub Stripe Coat' on special offer at £619.

By the time Arthur Morrison's novel was published in 1896, the slum had largely disappeared. It was torn down in one of the first clearance schemes of the London County Council. The solid, dour Boundary Estate was built in its place. At its heart, wonderfully but incongruously, is the grandest bandstand in the city, Arnold Circus, said to have been built on a mound of rubble from the demolition. The estate endures. A children's playground is reputed to mark the spot of a slum church which in turn was built on the Nichol's (or is it the Jago's?) most fetid and insanitary courtyard.

When I first started walking round the area — prompted by Morrison's novel — cheap furniture and veneer workshops still spilled onto the pavement nearby on Redchurch Street. The area had a down-at-heel feel aggravated by the dereliction on its edges, though the substance of the mansion blocks and a tolerably spacious design allowed it to escape the soulless monotony of so many of the East End's twentieth century estates. Much of the estate remains social housing, with a large Bangladeshi community. But an inner-city location so close to the cultural hotspots of Shoreditch and Hoxton was bound to become fashionable. A brace of estate flats knocked through to make a more spacious apartment now sell for £600k and more. After all they are, in a local estate agent's parlance, 'close to the galleries, cafes and boutiques of Redchurch Street and Brick Lane', where you find what were once pubs selling dishes such as salt-cured duck with kale and spiced brown shrimp butter.

Some of the old livelihoods of the area have found new life, more coincidence than continuity. Today the second-hand clothes shops are not last resort, but a first call for those seeking a retro look. The woodworking tradition is represented at the top end of Brick Lane by a shop-cum-workshop promising 'local craftsmanship at mass production prices' with edgy design and a young clientele.

Boundary Street itself has had the most remarkable makeover. A Terence Conran takeover. As you come out of Boundary Passage, and look ahead and to the right — look closely, though, for the luxury is not immediately on view — there's a warehouse that's been converted into twelve top-end hotel rooms and suites, three restaurants and a rooftop bar. And there's more. From a vantage point between the posts, on your immediate right stands (and I'm quoting from their design agency) a 'chic boutique'. On the left, an old cream and green tiled local pub is now the street-smart office of a creative agency. Its mission statement reads uncannily like twenty-first century speak for Morrison's literary purpose: to 'harness gritty stories and experiences to educate, inspire and unlock the true potential of young people'.

At the other end of the passage, the matching section of the High Street has not fared so well. It's stuck in a no man's land between the bright lights of Liverpool Street station in one direction, and in the other the galleries and delicatessens clustered round Shoreditch Town Hall. This stretch is blighted by buildings so drear they defy any attempt at gentrification. Where Shoreditch High Street meets Boundary Passage stands a sports bar and gentlemen's club, with a gaudy red neon sign which contradicts its name: 'Rainbow'. Even in the seamy world of strip joints, this looks sad. 'Our girls at rainbow', says the club's website, aimed at VIP customers and stag nights (not easily reconcilable, surely), 'are very friendly and like to get to know you as well as dance and teas [sic] you'. The style and the money are now on what was the slum side of the passage. It's the High Street that feels drab and decayed. The social geography of the 'Jago' has been turned inside out.

The marvel is that Morrison's 'Posties' survive. Every time I venture into this 'farther part of Shoreditch', I imagine demolition gangs will have brought low this last evocation of the area Arthur Morrison wrote about. Every time, I rejoice that it's still there — squat, undistinguished, but a tangible link with a commanding piece of literature and the London it represented. The historian Sarah Wise, author of *The Blackest Streets*, has argued that Morrison demonised the neighbourhood, partly for literary effect but also echoing his main informant, a self-publicising High Church cleric who sought to tame the Nichol. The novel was dedicated to this clergyman, and he appeared in its pages as a heroic figure. Yet novels create their own reality. Even those who grew up in the Old Nichol at times found it difficult to disentangle their childhood memories from the legend Morrison nurtured. More than any other London slum novel, *A Child of the Jago* has defined as much as depicted the locality in which it was set.

Observations – Leeds
Paul Barker

Commentary and reportage in the national media are ludicrously London-oriented. Things are getting no better. Regional newspapers are weakened commercially, and non-London TV has all but faded away. The BBC's politically-driven shift of some staff and programmes to Salford or Glasgow has made little difference.

In *New Society*, the magazine I edited from 1968 to 1986, we tried to keep a strong focus on the people who lived their lives many miles away from the metropolis: 'the other Britain'. We hoped it was a counterbalance. It was also a homage to admired forerunners like Mass-Observation, *Picture Post* magazine and the essays of George Orwell. In 1982, we published a collection of *New Society* essays, aptly called *The Other Britain*. In 2010, the V&A mounted a retrospective show of our documentary photos, called *The Other Britain Revisited*.

Meanwhile, in 1996, I was commissioned by the then-editor of the *New Statesman*, Ian Hargreaves, to write a weekly column which meant going out and about in 'the other Britain'; not sitting at my laptop, opining. The columns were called 'Observations' — the name of a much-loved section of *New Society*. The idea was to emphasis the virtues of keeping one's eyes and ears open; not rushing to political judgement.

The columns ran unbrokenly from May 1996 to January 1999. I learnt a lot. I hope readers did, too. I'm rather fond of the sample column (from 18 October 1996) that follows. I am a Yorkshireman, after all.

***

139

'This is the home of self-help, the land of the chip and cod, where the rag trade has turned into finance and finance has turned into God'

This is Samuel Smiles country, the land of self-help. The *Financial Times* once noted, with approval, that the Labour administration in Leeds ran its business with 'ruthless pragmatism'. Leeds used to be best known for its rag trade. This collapsed. But the city fathers and mothers did not sit down and weep. They got on with it. In Leeds, now, as many people work in finance as used to work in the rag trade. It has made a corner for itself in long-distance banking. The biggest firm on Headrow is now First Direct. Leeds has some of the largest commercial law practices in the country.

From this week the staff of these flourishing firms will have somewhere else to spend their money. Harvey Nichols has opened its first out-of-London branch on Briggate. It will do well. A *Vogue* writer remarks that Versace, crown prince of extravagance, is very big up North. The idea of 'dressing down' once you have made your money has little appeal. (Keep that for party-going in Islington and Notting Hill.) When you've got it, show it.

Yet part of the appeal of Leeds is that it remains very Yorkshire, very provincial. It was, fortunately, too conservative to get round to pulling down most of the city centre. (Unlike Bradford, whose mills supplied the cloth for Leeds's sewing machines.) Its character remains. Art editors constantly use its 19th-century town hall, with that bold stone turret, as the most recognisable symbol of local government.

The dark, romantic streetscapes of Atkinson Grimshaw – a grand, gritty name – in the City Art Gallery are still recognisably of the same Leeds, a hundred years after they were painted. The destruction wielded by an earlier version of ruthless pragmatism is mostly away from the city centre. Public health inspectors convinced themselves that Leeds's characteristic back-to-back houses were a life risk in themselves. In fact, the main trouble was that they had too many people in them and those people were too poor. Richard Hoggart's home territory of Hunslet is a sad sight: a motorway driven through it, and the housing torn down for the second time since the war. Nearby, Leeds' very own out-of-town shopping mall, the 650,000 square foot White Rose will open next year. The uses of prosperity.

Samuel Smiles, who lived in Leeds most of his life, is best-known for *Self-Help*. But he also wrote *Duty, Character and Thrift*. Leeds has taken to banking like a moor-hen to water.

On Quarry Hill, at the end of Headrow, stood one of the biggest, dourest council estates in Britain, modelled directly on German workers' housing. In its place you now have the West Yorkshire Playhouse and the grandiose post-modern palazzo of the National Health Service Executive. When the Department of Health decided to move so many civil servants out of London, it researched into the merits of rival cities. Leeds and Manchester ended up as the front-runners. Leeds won because its local economy was strong. (This was due to successful local enterprise, the report said. It was not due to Japanese, Taiwanese or Korean companies, lured by tax breaks, government grants and cheap labour.) Leeds was also perceived as a good place to live, close to open countryside. It had little inner-city dereliction. It had kept its interlaced network of Victorian shopping arcades.

If elected regional government every arrives in England, Yorkshire will be run from Leeds. The Government Office for Yorkshire — a one-stop shop for national bureaucracy — is already here, in a dreary block next to City Station. The architect was John Poulson. His career of corruption, recently evoked on television in *Our Friends in the North*, is a reminder, among so much talk of Tory sleaze, that Labour men are just as bribable. The pitiful thing was how little it took to bribe them.

141

Go under the railway bridge and you come to the River Aire. This is where the city is pouring its money in. New offices, new middle-class houses, new restaurants, and much evidence of what urban planners call the Arts and Culture Economy (ACE, for short): the new Royal Armouries museum, a Tetley Brewery museum. Leeds has caught museum-fever. Part of St James's teaching hospital will become a museum of medicine. Over in Guiseley there is talk of Harry Ramsden's opening a Fish and Chip Museum.

In both sorry and anger Hoggart gives chapter seven of *The Uses of Literacy* the heading 'Invitations to a candy-floss world'. I walk through the Victorian arcades, thinking about that. Mosaics show a spinner, a technical draughtsman, a miner and a symbol of learning. Leeds was the heartland of working-class self-help, also. In the 1950s, when Hoggart was writing, the university's evening classes were led by men too far left, and too maverick, to get jobs anywhere else.

There is an elegant new fountain in the arcade. A kiosk sells 'European bread': Bavarian Zwiebel Brot, Swiss High Fibre, Scandinavian White. Even before the arrival of Patsy's *Absolutely Fabulous* store, the shops in the 'Victorian Quarter' (the new public-relations name) included Hobbs, Oliver & His Armani Jeans, and Red or Dead.

Three tough-looking ten year olds drift up to the fountain with cans of shandy. Invitations to an Armani world. You pays your money and takes your choice. If you have the money, that is.

A Walk To Tafraoute
Sara Jane Palmer

The idea for these hangings started with a scorchingly hot walk in the clear bright dryness of the desert air in early April, through a flower covered rocky desert. We were walking towards a powerful group of large painted rocks five miles away — a natural series of massive rock formations that were painted by a Belgian artist Jean Veran in 1984. They still stand in the desert just south

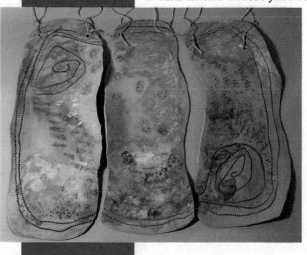

of Tafraoute in Morocco.

I used extremely dry glaze on high-fired clay, reminiscent of the gritty ochre and rusty sands and rocks of the North African desert. This series of triptychs is formed of white stoneware clay and painted freely with five or six

coloured slips; — red, blue, yellow, white and black that are sometimes visible

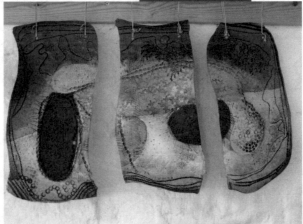

beneath the dry glazes and is a reference to the Painted Rocks.

The surface texture of the tiles is impressed with silver

144

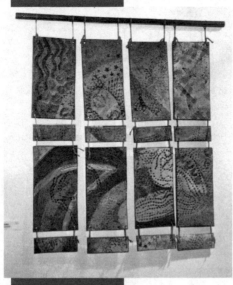

jewellery depicting the Southern Cross (from Morocco) along with beads, combs and shells. I wanted to include a reference to the importance of water sources and the position of the stars — both fundamental to the desert peoples, descendants of whom still live extraordinary lives on the fringes of the Sahara.

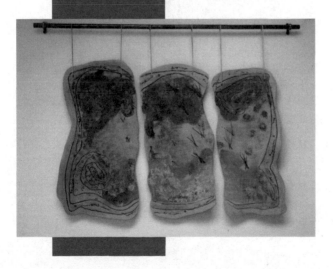

Additional slips are brushed on and the slabs left to harden. The tiles are cut and shaped and left to dry. They are then biscuit fired and brushed with natural oxides, then fired.

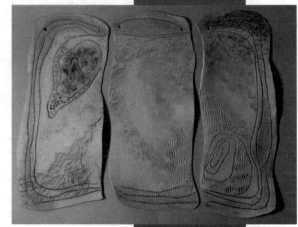

They are hung with silks on an oxidised copper pipe.

The *Guga* Men
Robert Macfarlane

Listen now. Listen now again to the singing of the *guga*
men out there on the bare rock of Sula Sgeir, hunched in
a stone bothy on that tiny island far out into the North
Atlantic, on a Sabbath fifty years ago. If I could sing it or
play it to you I would, but I cannot, so this will have to do.
The scene: a rough stone bothy, six feet high at its highest point, corbelled out of blades and blocks of shattered
gneiss, its cracks plugged with rags or with the warm
bodies of the Leach's petrels who nest here. In its centre
a peat fire, above which hangs by twine a storm-lantern,
lending light to the space; around the edges, rough stone
sleeping benches, on which the twelve men are huddled,
wearing tweed jackets, heavy wool jumpers. The spit and
chuckle of the fire. The wind moving outside, testing the
bothy.

Then the singing begins. First comes the leader, his
voice low and lilting, but powerful and rich, incanting the
verses of the day in Gaelic — *ach is e an gràdh as mò
dhiubh so*, 'and the greatest of these is charity...' — his
voice dipping and then rising again at the end of the
verse.

The lesson ends. A pause. A cough to clear the throat.
Then the leader offers a high sung line, from one of the
psalms, his voice rising in volume, pure notes but sung
from the throat or chest. This is the 'throwing' of the line,
its 'presenting'. And in like rhythm and metre, their
voices also raised in song, the other twelve men answer,
the sound filling and swelling the space of the bothy, one
or two of the voices dipping below to sing the low line of
the psalm. Another line is thrown, is followed, is completed. Shades in the sound of cotton-field southern
gospel, hints too of the muezzin's modulating call and of

the throat-singers of Siberia. Fire-songs of worship, consolation and comradeship. Song as devotion, but also as stay against the storm. These are the *guga* men of Ness, the gannet hunters, singing in the Year of Our Lord 1953.

Almost every summer for more than five hundred years a group of *guga* men have sailed to Sula Sgeir from Lewis in order to harvest the young gannets — the *guga*s, just on the verge of flying — from the cliffs of the island. A hard and dangerous voyage just to reach the island, when done alone under sail and oar. And then two perilous weeks on the islands itself, clambering down steep cliffs to reach the birds, carrying cudgels, organising the slaughter, building the pyre of *guga* bodies. Always a rest day on the Sabbath, of course. The men shelter and sleep in the bare stone bothies, wrapping rags around their heads at nights to stop the earwigs that infest the island from crawling in number into their ears.

Sula sits around forty miles due north of the most northerly point of the Isle of Lewis; the same distance from the Outer Hebridean coast as St Kilda. It is shocking terrain: a jaggy peak of gneiss, the topmost summit of a drowned mountain, a rotten black molar brawled over by surf, home to ten thousand gannets and to the only albatross in the North Atlantic. It is an experiment in geological brutalism. The sea has bored clean through the southern part of the island, forming a series of caves and tunnels. In big Atlantic storms, the waves break right over the top of rock, crashing against the unmanned lighthouse that warns ships to keep their distance.

Eleven miles to the east of Sula is its partner island of North Rona, yang to Sula's yin: a tilted green slab of smooth pasture, like a snooker-table collapsed at its southern end, which has been inhabited on and off for thousands of years by saints, farmers, shepherds and naturalists. St Ronan, one of the early Celtic Christian monks who dispersed themselves by the sea-ways, is supposed to have been the first dweller on Rona; arriving

there as part of his search for 'a place of his own resur-
rection' (in the phrasing of the *peregrini*). Ruins of a
chapel supposedly raised by him remain there.

On first sighting the two islands from sea, from the
south, it feels as if you have sailed into a parable. There
they are, forty or more miles out in the North Atlantic
and eleven miles apart. Implausible enough that land
should exist there, in the empty water between Scotland
and Iceland. And then that the contrast between them
should be so strong: green Rona, black Sula; fertile Rona,
brutal Sula. From a distance they appear more allegori-
cal than real: The Pasture and The Rock — a choice
offered to the seafarer. The earliest seafarers chose The
Pasture. St Ronan's sister, Brenhilda, is alleged to have
tried to live on Sula: she was found dead, so the story
goes, with a sea-bird's nest built inside her ribcage.
Lesson learnt; enough said. Since Brenhilda, Sula has
been left to the sea-birds, the seals, the fulmars, the
puffins, the gannets — and, briefly each summer, to the
guga hunters, the Men of Ness.

Ten men usually, sometimes a dozen. One of them the
leader. The first record of the hunt dates to 1549, when
the men rowed out in an open boat to cull the young gannets, and brought the bodies back as ballast. The
tradition continues today, with very little change. The
men now stay for two weeks each summer, usually in late
August. Landfall is made in the one possible landing-
place, in the main *geo* (bay) of Sula. But it is barely
feasible, being a steep slippery stone chute dropping at an
angle into the water. When there is any swell, the *geo*
becomes a choppy mass of waves moving in cross-
directions, bouncing off the walls, mashing together.
These days, the bothies are covered with plastic, then tar-
paulins, then netting, then weighted down with more
stones. Weatherproofing of a kind. The men continue to
share the bothies with the petrels who nest in the cran-
nies: tiny charcoal-coloured birds with white-flashed
tails, who spend all day at sea and come ashore with high

cries at night. Sometimes the birds land on the face of the sleepers and wake them up. The first day is spent setting up. Then the killing begins. The men are tasked with different jobs. They specialise: Fordism at work on the Rock. There are catchers, killers, scorchers, scrubbers, pluckers, pilers. The cliff-men head down, roped, on ledges slippery with guano, long nooses on poles, cudgels in hand. *Reach, noose, grab, crack.* The bodies start returning to the summit of Sula, where what is called 'The Factory' has been established. Two men singe the birds, two scrub the singed bodies to give them a smooth finish, three use the blowtorches, then their wings are chopped off, they are scrubbed again, then they are split open and emptied of their innards, and then their evacuated bodies are placed on the piece of functional art-work known to the men as 'The Pile', a sort of vast cairn of corpses, circular in shaped: mandala or pin-wheel. They give each other nicknames: 'Dodds', 'The Baby'. So it proceeds, for many days. On the middle Sabbath, a day of rest, prayer and song. If the storms come, they sit them out in the bothies; there is no working those cliffs with big waves about or in big wind. Once the work is done — hard days, long days — they sail south again, and crowds await their landfall at the Ness harbour. For each *guga*-hunter who has been out-aged by the island, who becomes too old to return, a cairn is built on their last visit. Seen from the sea the island's outline is prickly with cairns.

For centuries, the men went to Sula by open boat, rowing or under sail. 'There is in Ness a most venturous set of people who for a few years back, at the hazard of their lives, went [to Sulisker] in an open six-oared boat without even the aid of a compass', wrote the Reverend Donald McDonald in a 1797 census report. Now they go in big fishing trawlers: five hard hours, crashing north through the night to reach The Rock around dawn. The day and the hour of sailing is a well-kept secret — the *guga* hunters don't want the animal-rights protestors finding out. Even in a trawler, the weather needs to be on good behaviour. The last group of *guga*-men to reach Sula Sgeir under sail had done so in the summer of 1953, and they had sailed there in a boat called *Jubilee*.

Jubilee was a *sgoth niseach*: a class of Lewisian working open boat, lug-rigged and clinker-built, double-ended, designed for sturdy seaworthiness up there off the Butt of Lewis, where the Atlantic currents meet the currents of The Minch. Twenty-eight feet long, she had been built in 1935 by the MacLeod family from Ness and had remained a Ness boat for decades, before being re-registered to Stornoway. 'I have spoken to one of the men who last took *Jubilee* to Sula,' my Lewis friend Finlay MacLeod told me before I left for Ness, 'and he described being in the *geo* there in bad weather, and seeing her sides literally squeezed inwards by the pressure of the waves bouncing around there.' A watery vice, crushing and releasing, crushing and releasing.

It was the *Jubilee* that my friend Ian Stephen wanted to sail to Sula and back in this, her seventy-fifth year of life. He was eager to make this historic voyage, following the line of the *guga*-men, the line of a gannet's flight, to Sula and back.

Photograph by Michael Skelly

***

'Time for an hour or two of the dark arts', said Ian. He went upstairs and returned with three charts, a tidal atlas and what looked like a bright brass gannet's skull with a wine-cork on the end of its beak. He cleared half of the cluttered kitchen table, unrolled the charts, opened the tidal atlas, popped the wine cork off the gannet's skull and squeezed the hinged circle of skull, such that the points of the dividers — for this is what they were — first crossed and then became legs, with which he could stride across the charts.

Sea charts, even more than land maps, can lure you into hubris. All that featureless water — what could possibly go wrong? On maps of mountainous terrain, there are warnings: the hachures showing cliffs, the bunched contours indicating steep ground and fall-lines. Charts record headlands, skerries and mean depths of water, but because most sea-features are volatile — temporary functions of wind, tide and current — there is no way reliably of charting them. It is for this reason that the act of chart-reading, even more than most map-reading, is part data-collection and part occultism. Sailors, like mountaineers, practise their map-clairvoyance based on intuition and superstition as well as on yielded information.

I watched Ian run his fingertips over the chart, tracing out possible paths of sail, fathoming the future conditions of the sea based on memory and inference. *Given this wind, this boat, this crew... given that tide, given this tack....* The further you get from land, the longer you get into the journey, the more rapidly the hypotheticals multiply. *If we've failed to make this channel, that headland, by still water, by the turn of tide, we would have to have fled for here, or for there...* He read down through his fingertips, the chart's flat blues and greens popping up into relief: *The waves here, at this time, in these conditions, will be jabbly, unproblematic; but here they will stand up*

152

straight and hard like a wall. Wind-histories as well as wind-futures need to be taken into account, for the sea can have a long memory for past agitations. If a wind has blown hard from a certain quarter for days, the sea's motion will register continue to register that, even once the wind has dropped. It takes time to settle itself, to revise its inclinations.

The question preoccupying Ian was which sea-road to follow next. The plan was to sail out of Port of Ness on the far north of Lewis. From there, we would go either east round Cape Wrath and 'across the top' — the Pentland Firth — to Orkney: a thirty- to forty-hour continuous sail, that, one-way. Or we would sail north, pure due north, away up to Sula Sgeir and perhaps North Rona, a pair of uninhabited islands, hugely remote, forty miles out into the North Atlantic, but the sites of voyages and landings for millennia. Ian placed one hand on top of the other and laid them on the chart, then looked off into mid-air. The shipping forecast murmured on in the background: *Malin, Hebrides, Minch. Light southerly, 3 or 4. Cyclonic veering south-south-easterly for a time.* Good for a small boat. The ideal direction. Just a touch light, if anything.

In the end, it took an hour and half of scrying, assess-

Photograph by Michael Skelly

153

ing, plotting, second-guessing. The twisting march of the divider's legs, point by point, up over the empty ocean. The laptop offering detailed wind-forecasts. *Malin, Hebrides, Minch*. And then the portents aligned. Ian pinched the legs of the dividers together, pushed their sharp points back into the cork and laid them with a clunk across the chart. North to Sula Sgeir, the Gannet Island, it was.

Contributors

Chris Arnot is a regular contributor to the *Guardian*. He has also written for the *Daily Telegraph*, the *Independent* and the *Observer*. He co-wrote *The Archers Archives*. His essay here is taken from his forthcoming book on Britain's lost cricket grounds. www.chrisarnot.co.uk

Paul Barker, writer and broadcaster, was editor of the social affairs weekly journal, *New Society*, 1968-86. In 2006, Five Leaves published a new edition of *Arts in Society*, collecting essays by many *New Society* contributors. Paul Barker's book, *The Freedoms of Suburbia*, came out in 2009. His book on Hebden Bridge will be published next year.

David Belbin's Five Leaves' novel *The Pretender* is narrated by a precocious student who successfully fakes a Graham Greene short story featuring a prostitute from Nottingham. His *Bone and Cane* series (Tindal Street Press) is about Nottingham crime and politics. www.davidbelbin.com

Ross Bradshaw is the publisher at Five Leaves. He also jointly organises Lowdham Book Festival, www.lowdhambookfestival. co.uk.

Andy Croft's next book with Five Leaves is a novel in Pushkin sonnets, *1948*, illustrated by Martin Rowson. Together with W.N. Herbert and Paul Summers he wrote *Three Men on the Metro*, poems about the Moscow underground. His other books include a biography of Randall Swingler.

Gillian Darley's latest book is *Vesuvius*, published by Profile. She has written biographies of Octavia Hill, John Soane and John Evelyn. Her 1975 book, *Villages of Vision: a study of strange utopias*, was published in a revised edition by Five Leaves in 2007.

Richard Dennis teaches Historical Geography at UCL. His passions include mansion flats and model dwellings, bridges, trams, elevated trains and George Gissing, all of which feature in his book, *Cities in Modernity* (CUP), which explores modernity in the context of London, New York and Toronto, 1840-1930.

Roberta Dewa's essay is an extract from her current work in progress, a memoir, *The Memory of Bridges*. Her most recent published book is a collection of stories, *Holding Stones*, published by Pewter Rose. Roberta is currently working on a novel, *Home*. www.robertadewa.co.uk

John Lucas is the publisher at Shoestring Press, and is the author and editor of many collections of poetry and scholarly works. His most recent book for Five Leaves is *Next Year Will Be Better: a Memoir of England in the 1950s. 92 Acharnon Street* (Eland) won the Authors' Club prize for travel writing.

Robert Macfarlane's *Mountains of the Mind* won the 2003 *Guardian* First Book Award. He is a Fellow of Emmanuel College, Cambridge and the author of *The Wild Places. The Guga Man* is an extract from a longer work. His next book is *The Old Ways*, to be published by Hamish Hamilton in 2012.

David McKie was the deputy editor of *The Guardian* and continued writing the weekly columns 'Elsewhere' and 'Smallweed'. His books include a biography of the Victorian politician and swindler, Jabez Balfour, and *McKie's Gazetteer: a local history of Britain*. The article here began life as a related but different article in *The Guardian*.

Deirdre O'Byrne teaches English and Irish literature at Loughborough University, as well as Irish literature and the Irish language in various community settings.

Sara Jane Palmer is an artist making sculptural ceramics from her studio near Hadrian's Wall in Northumberland. She works with the human form, making heads, figures, wall-hangings, vessels and dishes. Her ideas are drawn from many places, classical sculpture, masks, Benin bronzes, Picasso, medieval art, icons, folk art, other representations of the human face. www.sarajanepalmer.com.

Ian Parks was made a Hawthornden Fellow in 1991. He is regularly published across the poetry world and beyond. His latest collection, *The Landing Stage,* is available from Lapwing. Several of his poems appear in the Five Leaves' Hull poets collection, *Old City, New Rumours*.

Mark Patterson is a freelance journalist, specialising in science and environmental/green economy articles. He is the author of *Roman Nottinghamshire* (Five Leaves) and runs the website www.romannottinghamshire.wordpress.com.

John Payne's most recent book is *The West Country: a cultural history,* published in 2009 by Signal Books. He is currently writing a book on Bath for the same publisher. His books for Five Leaves are *Catalonia* and *Journey Up the Thames: William Morris and Modern England.* A version of the essay included here appeared in *European Judaism.*

Iain Sinclair's 'Mr Tapscott' is an extract from his latest book, *Ghost Milk: calling time on a grand project.* A version of his *Guardian* essay, 'Man in a Mackintosh' formed the introduction to Roland Camberton's *Scamp,* published by Five Leaves/New London Edtions. www.iainsinclair.org.uk

Andrew Whitehead runs the *London Fictions* website www.londonfictions.com, which includes an article by Sarah Wise on Arthur Morrison's *A Child of the Jago.* He wrote the introduction to Alexander Baron's novel *Rosie Hogarth,* republished by Five Leaves/New London Editions in 2010.

Selected Five Leaves books
by contributors to *Maps*

Arts and Society
Edited by Paul Barker
Essays by Angela Carter, John Berger, Reyner Banham,
Michael Wood, Dennis Potter and others
306 pages, 1 905512 07 4, £9.99

Love Lessons
A young adult fiction novel by David Belbin
259 pages, 978 1 905512 70 6, £6.99

The Pretender
A novel by David Belbin
224 pages, 978 1 905512 51 5, £8.99

Secret Gardens
A young adult fiction novel by David Belbin
109 pages, 978 1 907869 22 8, £5.99

The Ghost Writer
"A rip-roaring read in Pushkin sonnets"
Andy Croft
82 pages, 978 1 905512 38 6, £7.99

1948
A novel in Pushkin sonnets
Andy Croft, illustrated by Martin Rowson
forthcoming in 2012

Three Men on the Metro
Poems by Andy Croft, W.N. Herbert and Paul Summers
121 pages, 978 1 905512 84 3, £7.99

Not Just a Game: sporting poetry
Edited by Andy Croft and Sue Dymoke
225 pages, 978 1 905512 13 3, £9.99

The Night Shift: a book of poetry
Edited by Michael Baron, Andy Croft and Jenny Swann
127 pages, 978 1 905512 58 4, £9.99

Villages of Vision: a study of strange utopias
Gillian Darley
339 pages, illustrated, 978 0 907123 50 7, £14.99

Next Year Will Be Better: a memoir of England in the 1950s
John Lucas
367 pages, 978 1 905512 91 1, £14.99

The Radical Twenties: writing, politics, culture
John Lucas
263 copies, 0 907123 17 1, £11.99

Things to Say
Poetry by John Lucas
76 pages, 978 1 905512 92 8, £7.99

Roman Nottinghamshire
Mark Patterson
297 pages, 978 1 907869 12 9, £11.99

Catalonia: history and culture
John Payne
2nd edition, 339 pages, 978 1 905512 82 9, £10.99

Journey Up the Thames: William Morris and Modern England
John Payne
224 pages, 0 90712368 6, £7.99

also

Scamp
A novel by Roland Camberton
Introduction by Roland Camberton
New London Editions
307 pages, 978 1 905512 94 2, £9.99

Rosie Hogarth
A novel by Alexander Baron
Introduction by Andrew Whitehead
New London Editions
367 pages, 978 1 905512 98 0, £9.99

Available from bookshops or, post free, from Five Leaves, PO Box 8786, Nottingham NG1 9AW, www.fiveleaves.co.uk